# Educating Youth in Missions

# EDUCATING YOUTH IN MISSIONS

Mildred McMurry

CONVENTION PRESS
*Nashville, Tennessee*

A publication of
WOMAN'S MISSIONARY UNION
Birmingham, Alabama



573-43602

Library of Congress Catalog Card Number: 60-9539
Printed in the United States of America
45.D5913

# Foreword

*Educating Youth in Missions* is second in the series of six books on WMU Aims which Woman's Missionary Union is publishing during the Baptist Third Jubilee Advance years—1959-64.

The missionary education of youth has been a primary concern of Woman's Missionary Union throughout its history. In this day of unparalleled world needs with matching opportunities for service, the education of youth in missions must be an expanding phase of WMU work. To that end Woman's Missionary Union invited Mrs. William McMurry to write this book.

Director of the Promotion Department of Woman's Missionary Union, Mrs. McMurry qualifies for this authorship by ability, education, experience, and belief in the missionary program of WMU. She is widely known throughout the Southern Baptist Convention as a forceful leader and a dynamic speaker. She earned her bachelor of arts degree at Tennessee College for Women and did graduate work at the University of Chicago.

Mrs. McMurry's knowledge of young people is extensive. She worked with them as a professional teacher in public school prior to her marriage, as a mother in the home, as a minister's wife in churches, and now as a staff member of Convention-wide WMU. In churches where her late husband was pastor she often served as WMU youth director and as a teacher or a superintendent in the Young People's Department of the Sunday school. During these years she was also a recognized missionary writer and leader. For six years she wrote the programs for *The Window of YWA* and was a contributor to the Intermediate Baptist Training Union quarterly as well as to *Royal Service.* She was mission study chairman for Tennessee Baptist Woman's Missionary Union for thirteen years.

The study of this book will bring to women renewed enthusiasm for educating youth in missions in our churches. It will establish more clearly in the minds of women in societies and leaders of WMU youth organizations the purposes underlying the program of our youth organizations and the responsibilities of women for these programs. It should result in greater interest in and development of the youth organizations in the churches.

ALMA HUNT
*Executive Secretary*
Woman's Missionary Union

# Contents

1. Youth in Today's World ..... 1

2. Looking at Youth ..... 16

3. Guiding Youth ..... 43

4. Youth in Woman's Missionary Union ..... 64

5. Youth and Woman's Missionary
Union Ideals ..... 103

Notes ..... 137

Bibliography ..... 139

Questions ..... 140

# 1

# Youth in Today's World

A grandmother and her five-year-old grandson sat close together in a big armchair. She had come to Chicago for an overnight visit primarily to see this little boy. After the custom of grandmothers she had brought him a gift—a beautiful book called *The Golden Geography.* As they sat together turning the colorful pages, they came to a map of the world. The little boy stopped his rapid turning and asked, "What's this?"

"It's the world, Bill," replied the grandmother.

With a quizzical look in his half-shut blue eyes he came back with, "What's it like?"

It's a good question. Young people are growing up in a world their elders have made. The leaders of today's youth have to bear a portion of the responsibility of adding to the problems and successes which they inherited from their generation. They cannot move out of the way of responsibility for what they have created; they are accountable to God and to youth. What, then, is today's world like?

*It is a small world.* In 1920, radio broadcasting began in the United States and England. Ships at sea, people in widely separated and remote villages, explorers in the Antarctic were able to make quick contact with other parts of the world.

The radio and airplane have completely changed man's idea about the size of the earth. During World War II they placed man closer to the people on the other side of the oceans than ever before. Whether he liked it or not he was living in a world community. Back in 1930 it took twenty-one days to get to Shanghai, China from San Francisco. In 1953 the distance from Japan to the West Coast was covered by air in twenty-one hours. By the end of the decade jet planes could fly from Los Angeles to New York in four and a half hours, from New York to London in five and a half hours, while experimental planes had attained a speed of 1555.98 miles per hour at an altitude of 45,000 feet. Television provided entertainment and aided education.

The demonstration of atomic power is the greatest scientific discovery of the time. The space age was born when Russia and America hurled into outer space satellites at 25,000 miles per hour and put them into orbit around the earth and sun. In 1959 the training for the first space man in the United States began in dead earnest, looking hopefully to the day when he would be put into earth-circling orbit. Where he goes from this achievement can be guessed only in part. Knowledge that atomic power has driven a submarine from the Pacific to the Atlantic under the Arctic Ocean's icecap is prophetic of what lies in the future. Our planet has indeed become small.

*It is a crowded world.* Each year more people are born than die. This is a fact nobody has disputed for centuries. The problem is that those who are born are living longer.

Medical discoveries and widespread advances in sanitation have improved health and lengthened life spans, thus lowering death rates. But birth rates have not gone down proportionately. The rapid expansion of the human family is described by the term "population explosion." The world's population is now growing by more than 47 million persons yearly. In 1960 the population exceeded 2.8 billion and by 1980 the estimated figure is 4 billion. In the year 2000 the population is expected to be near 6.5 billion.

The estimate by authorities in the field of population statistics is that the probable limit of the earth's ability to support people is about 7 billion. Young adults now twenty-five may live to see this estimate become reality. Survival of the human race is at stake. Three facts emerge which should be of concern to Christian workers with youth:

First, the spectacular growth in population has taken place in the underdeveloped countries that can ill afford the increase—Asia, Africa, the South Sea Islands, and virtually all of Latin America. More than half of the people in the world are underfed and more than half of the 90 million babies born in 1959 will be undernourished. These people are dissatisfied and are looking to see who will help them to improve their lot.

The second staggering fact is that the population increase is "producing the youngest population the world has ever seen." Most underdeveloped countries have more than 40 per cent of their total population under fifteen years of age. This is prophetic of a further increase in birth rates where the risks of death are rather low.

No Christian can be unmoved by the plight of starving human beings whose living standards continue to decrease by the pressure of increased populations. As long as two thirds of the world's people go to bed hungry every night they become an easy prey to communism. Christian leaders can help youth to see this picture of the world against the background of God's redemptive purpose. The impact of Christian faith can change the world mind if the seeds of faith are planted in the hearts of young people.

The third fact startling enough to sober every person who calls himself a follower of Jesus Christ is the knowledge that in the next forty years the number of Christians will decrease and the non-Christians will be steadily increasing. In the next forty years, according to authorities, the number of Christians may double yet "they will constitute a steadily smaller proportion of mankind." In 1960 non-Christians numbered approximately two billion. By 2000 the number is likely to be near five billion and the majority of them will be Asians.

In the thirteenth and fourteenth centuries the Mongols had built the widest empire known to man up to that time. It covered much of Asia and a part of Europe. A few Christians in Europe saw the pagan hordes as a great challenge and a mission opportunity, for their religion was of a primitive type which would yield easily to a higher faith. But these missionary-minded Europeans had little help from their fellow Christians; consequently, Asia became Moslem and Buddhist and remains so to the present time.

Today God is opening doors in these and other lands considered the strongholds of traditional religions. Like European Christians of another century, followers of Christ in America are being given an opportunity to carry the gospel into areas that may be lost forever if they are not entered *now*.

Today Christians make up 32 to 34 per cent of the world's population. Tomorrow they may number 22 to 24 per cent. Missionaries will be needed even more in the future than at the present. The youth in Baptist churches should know about the "population explosion" and the bearing it will have on missions in a few short years; for the missionaries of tomorrow sit in every Sunbeam Band, Girls' Auxiliary, and Young Woman's Auxiliary.

*It is a turbulent world.* The expressions, "The

world is in revolution," "The world is rapidly changing," are clichés but nonetheless true and underlie the upheavals that are in evidence all about us.

A dip into the past is necessary for a better understanding of one aspect of change which brought about the greatest freedom movement in history. Since World War II almost one third of the human race has achieved independence from colonialism. Twenty-eight new nations have come into existence since 1945. Africa is still struggling for her independence and is determined to be free of foreign rule and white domination. The revolution has affected some 900 million people in Asia, Africa, Latin America, and the Middle East.

In these millions surge the life and hope that comes with freedom. In spirit they are done with poverty, ignorance, and despair. They believe it is their inherent right to be free, to govern themselves in their own way. They do not want their resources exploited but, instead, used for the good of their own country. They are determined to achieve material prosperity and political status in one generation. No longer do they regard "things Western" as superior. These emerging people are conscious and proud of their nationhood and culture. They want to develop their way of life, to meet their needs in the light of modern knowledge.

Among the new nations, political revolution has pointed up two changes in attitude which have deep significance for Christian missions. With the decline of Western influence and in the countries where nationalism is strong, Christianity is looked on as a part of colonialism, a system which exploited the Asian and African for the benefit of the European. It is often referred to as "the white man's religion." This is easy to understand, for with the explorers from the Western countries went the missionary movement. In some of the new nations foreign missionaries are not allowed while Westerners are still permitted to enter. In the countries where the missionaries are allowed the people do not want their own religions denounced. If there is anything wrong with their beliefs they want to remedy it themselves.

With the birth of nationalism has come the resurgence of the traditional religions. There are competent observers who believe that the revival of these religions is an effort on the part of national leaders to unify the people and put them squarely behind the new government. It is a move to strengthen national unity.

This strong feeling of loyalty to their own nation and religion is one explanation of the reversal of policy in some countries where the missionary was once welcomed but is now only tolerated with no reinforcements being allowed.

For four centuries Western civilization spread throughout the world. Now its proud superiority is gone. Western Europe has been the center of what we were pleased to call Christendom. What now? A world civilization is being born. What will it be like? Two mighty forces are contending for the minds of these millions: communism and Christianity. Between the years of 1945 and 1959 communism made considerably more converts in Asia than Christianity. Unless the tide is turned the freeing of non-Europeans can mean world communism and added disorder.

*It is a tense and fearful world.* In forty years communism has gained control of one third of the human race. Dr. Frank Laubach says that on an average 100 million people have been turning to communism every year. Designed and nurtured by Communists the "hate wave toward America grows higher and draws closer." He predicts that by 1968 four fifths of the world will be Communist unless the trend is reversed. Communism thrives wherever people are hungry and government is unstable, corrupt, and weak. It has identified itself with the impoverished of the earth and has pledged destruction to the overfed and rich. It was out of such a background that communism came into being.

The freed peoples of the earth are battling poverty, hunger, and illiteracy. They are impressed by what they know of Russia's industrial progress, for in four decades she worked an industrial miracle and stands second only to the United States. Russia's background more closely resembles theirs than does that of the United States. They know that Russia also holds a commanding place in the world of politics; that she has emerged as a great military power and that these achievements have been realized within a generation. On the other hand the United States had both abundant resources and time in which to develop. The new nations have little of either. The United States holds half the world's wealth. These facts do not endear this nation to the rest of the world in spite of the financial aid that has been given to them. They have self-respect and do not want charity.

Russia and China have developed a plan for the indoctrination of Asian and African youth. Each year they bring into their respective countries 120,000 young people to be trained in the theory and practice of communism. These trained "missionaries" of communism return to their countries to tell the people that in Russia and China they have found the way and this is it: "Take everything from the rich class. The land and the machinery will be owned by the government. This will be distributed so that everybody will have enough and there will be *nobody* to oppress the poor."

Communism did not produce the world revolution but it has ridden the wave of violence. A part of communism's world strategy is to bring the new nation which has come out of colonialism into the communist orbit.

A discussion of the world situation today, no matter how fragmentary, is incomplete without reference to color and its relationship to anti-Westernism. During the centuries of colonialism when the West helped the East to have better government under supervision, improved ways of travel, and some of the benefits of Western education, the assumption was that the West was superior and that by patterning its ways of life after the West, the East could hope to raise its own standards. This attitude obviously revolved around a superior-inferior relationship. Through generations of control the peoples of the East have bitterly resented the West's attitude of racial superiority.

Closely related to the assumption of racial superiority is that of color. The man from the West is white; the non-Western is colored. The mark of colonialism, then, to the Asian and African is white domination over people of color.

To the Asians, Russia's imperialism in Eastern Europe is "different." To them it is the temporary occupation of one white country by another; a continuation of war in which European people seem to be endlessly engaged. Russia has been careful in her treatment of Asiatics and there is said to be no color discrimination in the country.

Africans and Asians feel closely akin to the American Negro. Carl Rowan,[1] distinguished American Negro journalist relates in *The Pitiful and the Proud* many experiences in India and Southeast Asia which illustrate this feeling of kinship. Meeting with a group of Indian correspondents from various sections of that country Mr. Rowan listened as one of them said:

I came because I saw your picture in the *Assam Tribune*. I looked at it and I looked at my dark hand and I said, "Here comes one of us," . . . We trust you and we speak frankly because there is a common bond of color . . . We are going to tell you some things we would not tell a white American. We resent your country dropping those atomic bombs on the colored people of Japan. We resent your atomic tests in the Pacific. If there is a dispute between a Western nation and an Asian nation, we automatically side with the Asian nation unless the evidence to the contrary is overwhelming.

Every unfortunate incident involving racial discrimination in the United States is played up in the newspapers of the world. The significant changes which have taken place for the betterment of race relations usually go untold. Be that as it may, Christian America should face up to the fact that there is nothing in either our Constitution or our religion that places a stamp of approval on color discrimination. The United States is looked on as a Christian nation and the principles on which it was founded are well known to the literate throughout the world. Southern Baptists, along with other Christians in America, are aware that treatment of the Negro in the United States has been one of the greatest hindrances to the effective work of the missionary overseas.

When Nikita Khrushchev came to the United States in September, 1959, there was no question about the sense of mission and dedication that motivated him. Over and over he said in one way or another, "We will bury you." Watching on the television screen his face "freeze with purpose, his little eyes flash," no one could doubt that he meant it. The challenge was primarily intellectual and spiritual. A dedicated Communist who believes that communism is a superior economic system and will replace capitalism as a better way of life, Khrushchev is determined to do all in his power to bring about total capitulation of countries of the world to communism.

Christians cannot be indifferent to the existence of communism as a way of life. Through viciousness and cruelty it has "deliberately fostered a real sickness of the human spirit by instilling in people's minds for its own purposes terror, suspicion, callousness, and the habit of brutality."

Nothing that Mr. Khrushchev said before the United Nations General Assembly about total disarmament indicated that he actually wanted the suspension of atomic tests to be further extended or to sidetrack any new competition in atomic testing. Hanson Baldwin, military analyst of the *New York Times,* made the statement that enough atomic weapons now exist to destroy the principal cities of Russia and the West, to leave large areas of the earth uninhabitable, to kill probably hundreds of millions of people. All-out military power today—unlimited and unrestrained—clearly implies the death of civilization as it is known today.

On atomic testing, Dr. George Kennan[2], distinguished diplomat speaking as a Christian, laid the matter squarely on Christian conscience in these significant sentences:

> Some of the scientists endeavor to reassure us that damages from radioactive substances have been negligible so far. Not *many* deaths, they say, can be expected to ensue from this increase in radioactivity compared with those which occur from natural causes. One scientist explained that if 100 people would be killed by the effects of a normal atomic explosion, then only 102 could be expected to die from the effects of the increased radioactivity.
>
> But whoever gave us the right as Christians to take even one innocent human life, much less 102 or 102,000? I recall no quantitative stipulation in the Sixth Commandment. God did not say through Moses that to take 102,000 lives was wicked but 102 was all right. I fail to see how any of this can be reconciled with the Christian conscience.

*It is a lost world.* Dr. William Hocking said that there is more widespread and deliberate lostness now than ever before; that man has found new ways of being lost. Only one is needed and that is the rejection of Christ. But modern man is being deceived by words.

There was a time when men cried out to the preachers, "What shall we do to be saved?" Few are saying that today but they are admitting blankness, frustation, meaninglessness at the center of their lives. They are not going to the preacher but to the doctor, the psychologist, the psychiatrist with confessions and questions. They are turning to cults, isms, and ancient religions, which do not hold up a mirror to man's sinful nature but offer compromises which are compatible with sinful nature. They are embracing communism as a promised way to create a new heaven and a new earth.

Jesus gave full allowance for the strength of wrong and the power of entrenched evil as soldiers laid their hands on him. "This is your hour and the power of darkness," he said. Evil is a mighty foe and holds in its grip more than two billion of the earth's people who lay no claim to any Christian faith.

The gospel is the cornerstone of our faith—Christ, God incarnate, who became sin and in the death on the cross made it possible for all mankind to be reconciled with the Father.

In his book, *In One Spirit,* D. Campbell Wyckoff writes "The day has passed when Christians thought of missions as concerned largely with the conversion of persons from non-Christian religions in faraway lands. Today there is a worldwide paganism in evidence in all nations including the United States."

This paganism is shown in obsession with things, the desire to get hold of material possessions at the expense of the individual or society as a whole. This knowledge makes home and foreign missions one great mission of Christendom. In order to expedite the work there must be boards of missions charged with specific areas but the purpose is the same: to show forth God's redeeming love in Jesus Christ.

It is with this knowledge and against the backdrop of the times that Woman's Missionary Union must undertake to educate youth in missions.

# 2

# Looking at Youth

Many wonderful discoveries have been made in the twentieth century, but none is so great as the discovery of the child. It is in this century that he has come to be looked on as a person—not the elongation of papa and mamma, but an entity within himself to be treated with respect, loved, given a place in the home and church as a human being. Jesus set forth this truth nineteen centuries ago when he placed a child in the midst of his followers and said, "Suffer the little children to come unto me, and forbid them not: for of such is the kingdom of God." In this way the Lord was saying to future adults, as well as to his followers then, that during the years of childhood minds and hearts can be turned either toward God or away from him. The cause of missions depends on the training of youth.

Students of youth development have done research over many years and have made their studies available in books and magazines. Leaders and teachers of missionary education have found the results of these investigations of superlative value.

Many leaders still believe that a child is to be

seen and not heard; that his mind is a simple vacant vessel into which a leader has only to pour what she knows to make him into a missionary-minded youth. There is a need to understand that information divorced from the child's life is soon forgotten by him; that a child's mind is not simple and it is far from vacant.

To help the child grow into a missionary-minded adult, the methods used in teaching him about missions should follow accepted educational methods and principles. These principles point out that a child learns more quickly and happily when the teacher discovers his world of natural interests and desires; that a knowledge of the general characteristics of the age which she is to teach is a prerequisite to that discovery. Such an understanding on the part of the teacher is necessary in leading and guiding youth, whether of Sunbeam age or a young woman on the threshold of adulthood.

### Laws of Growth

It is well to remember that the laws of growth, and approximate age at which certain changes take place, are rough estimates, for every child is an individual and has his own law of growth. Changes not visible to the eye are continually going on inside a child. This is God's design for growing up. Dr. James Hymes[1], international authority in the field of elementary education, warns:

"Once you make the general guides too definite

. . . you put pressures on youngsters for accomplishments they cannot yet do. The children become worried and tense along with you . . . growth makes the actual decision: a process which neither child nor adult touch. You cannot be looking at a calendar. You cannot be looking at an average. You have to watch each individual."

At every age youngsters can learn to do some things but they cannot, others. It is not because they do not want to try or that they are lazy. Success depends on their growth. This is a law—God's law written deep in the body, mind, and emotion of each child. To be a successful leader of youth the adult must know something about these laws of growth and abide by them.

*Birth Through Eight*

A child inherits his rate of growth. There is nothing he or the leader can do about it; therefore, the child has to be himself. There is no use trying to speed him up or slow him down. Whenever this is done he is hurt and permanent harm is done. The time will come when the child is ready. The three-year-old likes to listen to a story but reading is the adult's concern, not his. The same is true of most four- and five-year-olds. They can neither see nor think well enough. But the wheels are turning inside, as Dr. James Hymes expresses it.

Development is a slow process. Yesterday the baby gurgled but today he said a word. Yesterday the year-old stood and rocked back and forth; today he took a step. Yesterday the thirteen-year-old would wear nothing but jeans; today she preens before the looking glass in her first evening dress.

Children are always ready to learn something but they must like it. The baby in the bed is ready to learn—to see more, to grasp better, to reach. The toddler is not defying the adult when he refuses to eat with a spoon or stand alone. He cannot, for his muscles have not developed sufficiently for him to perform these physical acts. His coordination is in the earliest stages of development. He needs time.

When a child is interested the leader may be sure that he is learning. If he is bored and unresponsive she may be reasonably sure that she is giving him something he is not ready for or she has not provided the situation which makes him want to learn. Interest is a gauge that shows if the teaching is timed perfectly with the child's growth. It shows in his face. He asks questions; he listens; he gives time to whatever has aroused his interest. He does not forget. When a child is interested he does not mind working. He is tireless in his efforts and will give the job everything he has. Getting out the blocks or putting up the paints are not chores. They are attached to interest when the timing is right for the child.

Once a leader has found the child's interest it is not necessary to "make it easy." He will hold to a high standard if the leader does. In the earlier years the adult knows that she must help the child to keep his doing in line with his physical growth. There often comes a time when the leader has to say, "That's all for now."

A child is everlastingly on the go. For a long span of years a child must be active. If the leader gives him enough space and then lets him move physically and mentally with his hands and feet, his tongue and mind, there will be little trouble. This characteristic of the child is not a peculiarity that can be handled during a few minutes of playtime, but it is the very core of his being.

Touch a baby's foot and he is in motion all over; hold before his eyes a red ball and his feet and legs go into action. The development of ability to control his movements is a slow process. A one-year-old can localize movements better than a baby six months old. Three-year-olds have more control than two-year-olds. A Junior-age youngster has still more control. A child psychologist[2] points out that long years of growing are needed before the nervous system matures so that the human being does not have to throw all of himself into everything that comes along every minute of the time.

### The Preschool Child

From birth to junior high school age the child is not too far from the beginning of this long journey to adulthood. The leader of Nursery-age children must know that they have to be in motion; they crawl, run, jump, touch, move almost constantly, and say whatever comes to their minds. They thrive on minimums of sitting, listening, being quiet, and letting others do it. The same perpetual motion marks the four- five- six- seven- eight-year-olds. The chief difference is in the amount of noise they make. This increases with each year. It is difficult to say when it reaches the maximum point!

The *child* is in the center of everything he does. He cannot help being; it is his nature. The infant's world is his bed, his room, his parents. He likes a story that counts *his* toes, *his* fingers, names the clothes *he* wears, garment by garment; lists the food, item by item, that *he* had for breakfast or lunch or dinner.

He listens when he is told where he has been and describes what he saw. As he grows older he is able to see a little more to the right, to the left, and up and down. His eye-span is circumscribed by the law of physical growth and he quickly sees all there is to see for him. But he is still in the middle of what he sees. His hearing is acute. He loves sounds but not harsh ones. He responds to the soft voice, the quiet step, the flowing person rather than the running-into-everything kind.

Anything that throws light on *him* is important. He lives in the present, not in the future, and even the *now* is of concern only as it relates to himself.

The preschool child wants his own way. Every act is an effort to prove himself. If he is allowed to assert himself within reason, when he gets older his feeling of importance will not be demonstrated in assertive ways. He will not grow into a power-motivated adult. The child who has been allowed to prove himself, usually has known love and understanding; his normal, natural drive for importance has not been blocked but has been allowed to express itself in guided play and work.

Wanting to feel big, to be at the center of things is not confined to the preschool age; it goes on and on and grows bigger and bigger if it is not recognized as part of normal growth. If there are to be future accomplishments every human being must feel that he is important. In knowing oneself, in thinking of oneself as highly as he ought, both ancient philosophy and Bible truth are in harmony. When a child gets this awareness of himself at home and in the beginning years at school he will not feel the need later to push others around in an effort to prove his worth.

### *Four Through Eight*

Children four through eight have advanced from the stage of putting together simple puzzles to building airplane models; from counting "one," "two," and "many" to adding simple figures with ease; from playing alone or side by side to participating in group games; from a meager understanding of the past and future to recognition of distance and time.

The younger child has little understanding of money as to size and value. At eight he is familiar with various pieces of money, can make change for simple amounts and is beginning to learn what money can buy. This is the age for the lemonade stand in a corner of the front yard. It is a good thing for an eight-year-old to have an allowance. At four he is in the process of learning to share, take turns and to ask for what he wants. When he is eight he is outgoing in his manner, will share materials and toys and will ask for rather than take the things that he wants.

Socially and mentally the fives, sixes, sevens, and eights have come a long way. Although the eight-year-olds still play together as do the younger ones, the boys and girls often separate and play against each other. From this point forward their interests are colored by sex. For the first time he is beginning to desire a "best friend" of the same gender. Eight-year-olds have begun to enjoy reading. Books provide him with answers to many of his questions. They are beginning to find satisfaction in learning about other people.

*Spiritual growth.* The child begins his growth spiritually the moment the mother takes him in her arms after birth. That very instant, for it is then that he feels love. If he is not wanted, at precisely the same moment his growth toward God is retarded. The very young child "thinks" only with his senses. As his experiences grow he can be led through the beauties of nature into the knowledge that God made the flowers, the trees, the grass, the soil. He learns that he can talk to God and thank him for the things he sees and knows. He can have worship experiences, feeling that God is near.

"What are you doing?" called a mother to her young daughter.

"Just sitting out here on the steps with God," she replied.

The sixes, sevens, and eight-year-olds ask many questions about God. They are growing in their knowledge of him. They have observed the church ordinances of baptism and the Lord's Supper; they want to know the meaning. There is a growing concern about death and heaven. The older children like to look in the Bible for familiar verses and learn them quickly.

The eight-year-old knows the difference between right and wrong. His conscience is sensitive. It is not unusual for a child at this age to feel conviction of sin. With guidance he may acccept Christ as Saviour and become a member of the church.

### *Juniors*

There is no hard and fast line between the Primary and Junior child as the previous discussion has indicated. The girls from nine through twelve, however, have certain general characteristics which are important and very necessary for the good counselor to know.

Juniors are *active*. They do not like to *sit*. They usually go to sleep if an adult attempts to hold them with words alone. "Tongue wagging is not enough activity to keep them alert."[3] It is easy to misunderstand this characteristic of the Junior who does not have to shout and run to be active. The mind is as active as the body. There are things to make, stories to act out, drills to engage in, pictures to draw, games to play that require thinking. This is the age of the quick memory. What is learned during these years is generally retained. The Junior girl is beginning to change physically, particularly in the eleventh and twelfth years. Self-consciousness and moodiness may show at this age. Her reactions may be unpredictable.

Juniors are *curious* about everything. Someone has said that the Primary child is learning to read while the Junior is reading to learn. The Juniors want facts. "Is this a true story?" they ask. They have left the fairy tale behind. In discussing two series of historical books with a twelve-year-old, an adult learned that the youngster preferred the book telling the historical event straight without the guise of fiction. When he was asked why, his reply was, "I can't tell what's so and what isn't when it's a story." The "true story," even if it is history, can be made as dramatic as any piece of fiction.

Asking "why" begins as soon as the child can talk. The only difference now is that the questions are more nearly related to the Junior's expanding knowledge and awareness of his physical world.

Junior-age boys and girls have a *sense of fairness*

*and justice.* There is no better time to lead them to develop attitudes of sharing and accepting other children as they are. They resent the trampling down of any child for no reason which they can understand. The wise leader meting out justice with impartiality to all children alike will be given confidence and respect.

Obedience should be based on truth and justice. The lack of either on the part of parent or leader is to court disaster. If the demand for obedience is inflexible the result will be lack of originality and independence of ideas. Later in life it will show up in a lack of conviction. It is essential that the child be led to see that recognition of authority and obedience to law are roads to happiness and satisfaction.

When a girl reaches the age of nine she begins to live more outside the family and its influence. She notices other adults besides her parents. Unconsciously she is patterning her life after those around her from the books she reads and the stories she hears or sees on television. During the highly imitative period, for the child's sake, adults must be what they want the child to become. Now is the time to expose her to people, real or imaginary, who are worthy of imitation.

The Junior is developing leadership qualities. She likes to hold an office and if given the opportunity she will without self-consciousness quickly nominate herself for the chief place. A mother on being told by her daughter that the time for the election of officers in the Girls' Auxiliary was nearing said,

"I think it would be a good thing if you thought about which girl would make the best president and vote for her." The daughter candidly replied to her mother,

"I don't have to think about it. I want to be president myself." With a little coaching these girls can become effective officers.

The Junior is susceptible to religious training. More adult church members testify that they accepted Christ at this age than at any other. The Junior deserves to receive the best possible instruction from her home and church. Her natural curiosity and growing knowledge lead her to think about the physical world and how it came to be. Her developing conscience and the feeling of what is right and wrong lead her into an awareness of sin. This is called the "age of accountability."

When the child has passed from the state of innocence to the state of moral discernment he becomes aware of his need for God. Now is the time when he can most easily be led to accept Christ. If the atmosphere of the home has been Christian throughout his life, it is not difficult to lead a Junior to think of God as a just and wise Father who will give a girl or boy the joy of working with Him to make this a better world. Many missionaries, pastors, and leaders testify that they heard God's call when they were Junior age.

*Intermediates*

The name itself is suggestive of the time of life: the between period, the period between childhood and maturity. This is the age of adolescence when the boy or girl is "neither fish nor fowl nor good red herring." The young person is in the process of becoming a mature adult. It is a turbulent time of life not only for himself, but also for everybody associated with him, unless he is understood. But it can be a time of full living and continual self-discovery.

Many educators and scientists who have made studies in the field of adolescence divide the ten or twelve years into three periods: early, from twelve to fourteen; middle, from fifteen to seventeen; and later, from eighteen to twenty-five. Again it is well to call to mind that these are not fixed boundaries, but it is valuable to know something of the general characteristics of the adolescents so that the leader may know what to expect and how to plan.

*Early adolescence.* The most outstanding fact of early adolescence is rapid physical growth. Girls grow faster than boys but the boys quickly pass girls in size and weight. Rapid growth brings on awkwardness, self-consciousness, and shyness. Boys and girls become sex-conscious at this age. These strange and new emotions, wonderful as they are, may become troublesome without understanding help. Psychologists warn parents and leaders of youth that these intense emotions and responses are not to be played with or laughed at.

At ten the average girl thinks every boy thirteen is a nuisance; at sixteen the boy becomes a dreamboat. But take him seriously no matter what he looks like! At different times in a young girl's growth she needs different satisfactions. They are a part of her, built in, so to speak. Needs are fundamental. The adolescent at this stage alternates between periods of intense activity and complete indolence. She expresses herself often in crude ways and is impatient with adult opinions and concerns. "Put on your overshoes. Don't go out in the rain without your raincoat," are greeted with disdainful shrugs, perhaps the slamming of the door, or a sputtered, "I'm no baby. Aw, skip it." Wise elders look on these reactions as symptoms of growth, not insolence or delinquency.

The power of thought and choice is greatly increased; intellectual interests are broadening. As they go along, these young people are working out rules of living though they may not recognize what they are doing. Their standards of judgment of others are severe. They have very little sympathy with the mistakes of others. This unbending attitude toward what they have accepted as right and wrong leads them into conflict with those who may be acting contrary to their ethics.

Socially they are organized into small groups that rule their activities strictly, even harshly. This is the age of the gangs which may become a menace if left alone. They have a difficult time being successful with adults but they are struggling to find a place and be accepted in the social order. Gangs, clubs, small groups can provide a place of acceptance and approval which are necessary to the in-betweens.

This is the age for the beginning of hero-worship, daydreaming, and building air castles. The early adolescent is in the process of developing toward an ideal. She will never be surer of herself than now. This is commonly called cockiness, which is often a pose to cover up insecurity. She may falter (and when she does, needs adult support), but she is able to make plans and carry them through. Even then she may show resentment, but underneath she is devoted and lovable.

*Middle adolescence.* Because of difficulties in separating ages normally considered middle adolescence, this period includes the Intermediate girl in her last year in Girls' Auxiliary and the first two years after her promotion into Young Woman's Auxiliary.

Boys and girls at this age find themselves now equipped with the full powers of sex but not with full understanding of its power. They are both delighted and dismayed with their bodies. Daydreaming is now almost an occupation with self as the hero or heroine. The new-found power is often expressed in the urge to create through writing, art, and music; it is frequently noted in restlessness they do not understand.

The adolescent girl of this period has to make

many social adjustments. She sees people clearer than ever; she experiences sympathy for others in trouble or illness. It is a time of idealism. Still rebellious against adult restrictions, she is beginning to adopt adult standards of behavior; to look at life as a whole. It is not easy, takes time, and she has to mull over it. She is still giving attention to the present but is also looking upon the near-future. Her real problem is to get through the next situation successfully. It may be a senior English book report, a coming-up date, a YWA program to plan, a money crisis to meet. She is beginning to think about—after high school, what? Imagination takes a very practical turn.

This is a time of fierce independence of adults in general, though she may lean heavily on certain of her adult leaders. It is a time of interdependence with friends of her own age. The gang spirit is still strong.

The adolescents at this age are in senior high school. They are capable of taking their places as responsible members of the community. Frequently a town, city, or church has Youth Week. The youth take over the municipal government for a day or a church's activities for a week. Responsibility is reflected in other ways: their discovering neighborhood needs in a social science class, taking part in home projects, talking over community problems, and discussing political issues with adults. It is to be expected that much of this investigation is by trial and error, but for the first time the adolescent is enjoying new experiences and being entrusted with responsibility without the protection of adults.

Young people at this age are "like their own hot-rods . . . full of power, half-equipped, and seldom under control."[4] But they are on their way! The world is at dawn . . . completely wonderful.

*Later adolescence.* Before the end of this period youth come to complete physical development. The sex powers are at their height. Marriage is likely to take place. Settling down and going "steady" with one person is the usual social pattern. How grown-up they are is now measured in terms of behavior. The youth who diets to make the basketball team or works tirelessly to get on the college paper or the debating society or win a place in a glee club, orchestra, or play is learning self-control and imposing self-discipline. The thinking and behavior of these young people reflect some sort of philosophy of life which they began working on in middle adolescence. How do they look at life? If they have had the right kind of guidance, at its center is faith in God and commitment to a principle of serving others.

In later adolescence, leadership has been discovered and, to some extent, trained. This is true when adults have allowed youth to assume leadership at whatever age it has been demonstrated. If an adolescent says, "I'm just a slave living under a dictatorship; they are always telling you what to do," it is glaring proof that initiative has been curbed and somebody is responsible for checking the potential that God deposited in that life.

In this summary of childhood and adolescent development the adult leader of youth has looked at their most conspicuous characteristics. The youth will bring all of these traits—every one of them—to every meeting of Sunbeam Band, Girls' Auxiliary, and Young Woman's Auxiliary. They will not leave part of them at home, drop off a few more at school, park others on Sunday in the various departments, but will hustle the whole personality right on to the weekday missionary meeting.

### Break Loose Is Normal

In this age of the "Organization Man" when the adult is emphasizing conformity and not human differences, there is justification in looking again at the adolescents. This is the time when the expression of their fierce independence of adults takes on the character of revolt.

Rebellion among youth is not unique to the twentieth century; it is only more dangerous and serious in this day of crowded highways and powerful automobiles. Violence has become commonplace in the comic books, on television, and at the motion picture theatre. Youth is bombarded with movies and TV programs which depict easy success and easy money. It is little wonder that they are having difficulty in growing to maturity in a world where their integrity is being softened and society seems bent on destroying them. Revolt is inherent in their nature and is God's preventive against too many curbs during the crucial period of development when they build self-esteem and learn to test society's rules and themselves.

The conduct of youth in every period of history is shocking to their elders. A minister wrote:

"It is too true, frightfully, miserably true that there is not the same reverence for parents as there was a generation back; that the children break loose from their parents, spend their parents' money, choose their own road in life, their own politics, their own religion, alas! too often for themselves; that young people presume to do and say a hundred things which they would not have dreamed in old times."

These words might have come from any pulpit in the land as recently as last Sunday. Actually the sermon was preached by Charles Kingsley in England and published in 1858.

### *Idealism Hoodwinked*

After World War I, youth on the continent of Europe as well as in America broke away from the restrictions of the school, the church, and the home. The youth of this land had been hoodwinked into believing that by fighting they could "make the world safe for democracy" and settle all international problems. All youth had gone out to fight in defense of ideals they held sacred and to establish justice. But justice was not established and the world seemed no nearer democracy than before. These young people believed that there must be a better way than the adults had shown them.

Revolt was particularly strong in central Europe and among German youth. Though there were many youth organizations with many purposes in Germany, they all held in common a revolt against conventional authority.

All around the world there were evidences that youth was rallying for a purpose other than war. They had set for themselves the task of finding sources of national strength, apart from a materialistic emphasis, which had been lost preceding and during the war. Once again youth was expressing faith in spiritual values. Hopes were high. Then something began to happen all over again. Men in places of national leadership were up to their old tricks. Greed and a lust for power once more lifted ugly heads. Youth was again seduced.

It was harder a second time to muster the forces of youth to take up arms in a cause which seemed doubtful at the outset. The freedom bells had a hollow ring. Today there are no illusions among youth regarding a third war. There will be no permanent reconstruction after the H-bomb. There will be nothing left to settle.

### *Youth Versus Parents*

Regardless of world crisis or the tempo of the day, there has always been friction between young people and their parents. It is impossible for youth to look at things as their parents do. And it is very hard for parents to remember how things looked to them when they were young. Fifty years ago teen-agers were saying, "My parents try to run my life." "I wish mother would quit asking me where I've been and what I've been doing." "Father, why can't I have the horse and buggy to take Jane to the ice cream supper?"

How is this different from the present-day daughter who complains, "Why won't you let me do anything on my own? I'm too old to be a squab and too young to be a chicken. I must be a dead duck."

Or the son who says: "My dad keeps quarterbacking me and my mom wants me to do everything without *any* reminding. You don't know if you're expected to be eight or eighty. It's rough."

Parents of all ages have been bewildered by the teen-ager. This is nothing new. Dorothy Baruch[5] states it this way: "We worry when we feel a child of ours is growing away from us. We are bewildered still when we see him manifesting traits of which we disapprove. We ask ourselves anxiously, what makes him so moody. What makes him standoffish? Too forward? Too timid? Why does he look down on us and tell us virtually that we know nothing? . . . What about his confidence in us? Just yesterday, it seemed he depended so on us. Today perhaps a little. Tomorrow not at all. For what is he searching when he wanders away?"

During these transition years youth are searching for what they have always looked—a place to put down their roots outside the family circle. If they are too deeply rooted in dependence on their parents they will never achieve independence. If parents have given teen-agers religious faith out of which grows personal integrity, they will be able to plant themselves as acceptable, responsible persons in every relationship throughout life. Parents want their children to grow up, and they will if they are fully accepted in the home as they are.

Usually the leaders of our youth organizations are parents. They need to remember that "the drives, wishes, and fears" which motivated them in their youth are the same drives, wishes, and fears which youth of today possess. Johnny didn't turn over the chair in the Large Group Activity to spite the leader. Mary hasn't failed to learn her Forward Step material because she wants to be a failure or make the teacher appear to be a failure. Carol did not lose her copy of *The Window* and come unprepared to the YWA meeting to create a problem. These behavior experiences which are not readily understood by the leader are age-old. Leaders who can look at the young person's behavior and recognize it as growing pains normal for his or her age will feel less on the defensive, more sympathetic, and considerably more objective in handling him. The action of a child or youth in the organization may cause the leader to recall now how she acted when the reins were held too tight. Parents have always had the capacity to forget what they needed when they were young. As a teen-ager expressed it, "Parents are people who try to help you but don't know you well enough to do so."

There are reasons other than an age difference, easily recognized and logical, for the gap between adults and young people.

Youth spend more time outside the home than the parents did. This is true of children as well as of teen-agers. For the younger members in the family there are the extracurricular activities linked with school; there are clubs such as Scouts and Brownies; in small towns, the vacant lot or a neighbor's big yard; in larger towns and cities, amusement parks and community playgrounds within easy reach of the child's home.

Youth have had broader experiences than their parents had when they were young. The automobile, train, and airplane have reduced distances and made travel commonplace. In work, through movies, in general community contacts, and on the television set the youth are exposed to different standards of living which may be at variance with those of the home. They meet people whose ideas and ideals are in conflict with those held by their parents.

There are more places of amusement today, to tempt youth away from home. Many of these offer unwholesome stimulation in drinking, petty gambling, and reading of questionable magazines. Conflicts in what is right and wrong follow, confuse, and make for serious trouble.

*The Beatniks*

A segment of youth society called the "blue-jeans-and-leather-clad rebels" bore other names in the twenties and predepression days. The chief difference is that the jargon spoken by the so-called young intellectuals in the dingy cafes and bars of the big cities at the turn of the decade has become Japanese instead of French. These young people who call themselves beatniks have become mystics over night. It is chic to experience visions while listening to jazz or while riding in subways or on fast freight cars back and forth across the country. It is equally fashionable to meditate in groups or alone at home, "practicing how not to act and not to think." The beat generation has fallen for Zen Buddhism as their elders did in their day for Theosophy, a form of mysticism, which ceaselessly attacked Christianity and scattered the doctrines of reincarnation, nirvana, and the like as far back as 1875.

"This is a result of more than fifty years of effort on the part of Buddhist and Hindu missionaries in the metropolitan centers of America. Shortly before the turn of the century a steady stream of Oriental religious philosophers have visited, lectured, and made converts in this country."[6] The United States Buddhists have formed an American Buddhist association with headquarters in Chicago, Illinois. No doubt the Zen fad with its easy morality and denial of one God will pass, but there will be evil consequences reflected in many lives now and in the future. Like a previous generation, the beatniks have rejected the whole Judeo-Christian tradition which they do not know "in favor of that which they do not understand."[7] Only the name is new in this fad of present-day youth.

*Revolt Redirected*

Youth is deeply interested in the social scene. They have been prepared for this interest in greater measure than were their parents. Widening experiences and studies in public schools have contributed to such an interest. With younger brothers and sisters they see and know what is happening through radio and television by the time it occurs in almost any country of the world. Books about people and places are produced in abundance in exciting, beautiful formats. Public libraries, rental libraries, bookmobiles, and like means have made communication of ideas swift and within reach of all.

Major issues of today, such as labor and management relationships, migrant problems, corruption in politics, gangsterism, human suffering in every area of life on every continent, race tensions, issues between branches of our government appeal to and challenge youth. In the discussion of these social problems young people often find themselves in conflict if not in open revolt with their parents.

Youth has always possessed idealism. It is ageless. Whether in bibical times or in today's world they dream their dreams. Someone has explained it this way: "A youth is old enough to be aware of the ancient ills of human society and not old enough to have learned from bitter experience how stubbornly these ills resist human efforts to change them."

In suffering disillusionment during and between wars, youth has revolted against power-politics, the magnifying of superficial differences between nations, and the overemphasis on the superior judgment of adults who rarely admit they are wrong. Youth has always protested the mouthings by adults of Christian virtues which they do not practice.

But idealism persists. To listen to students giving their arguments in school clubs and debating societies is to know this. In every land they are filled with political idealism and ideas of international brotherhood. Students call on their governments to stop aggressions; they are on the side of independence movements and nationalism in all parts of the world.

Youth faces the problem not only of making a new civilization but giving that civilization a new life of spiritual values. Whether the youth of our land are consciously aware of the seriousness of the international situation, they are conscious of tensions and suspicions which surround and rob them of security.

Still idealistic, youth ask what they can do to bring about *real* peace in the world. It has been proved that financial assistance can not do it; that efforts at disarmament will not do it. Alliances and treaties will not do it. To generate hate by more hate produces only armed watchfulness.

In order to have peace as a ruling force in the world it is necessary to change the hearts of men. Man has been able to bring about many changes in nature by his knowledge of the laws of botany, physics, biology, and chemistry but he has not been able to change himself. Only God through Christ can do it.

To know that one can have a part in taking or in sending this good news around the world is the answer to youths' revolt against the tyranny of a materialistic age and their quest for peace in their own hearts.

"There's nothing to live for," cries youth.

"There's the gospel!" parents and leaders exclaim.

Now is the time to present the challenge of Christian missions!

3

# Guiding Youth

The success or failure of the youth program in missionary education rests not so much on youth as on the adults who are responsible for the leadership. They need to face their leadership not only against the backdrop of present world conditions and a knowledge of what youth is like but also with a willingness to look at themselves through the eyes of those they lead.

### *Youth Looks at the Leader*

In a questionnaire submitted to a group of young people in summer school and reported by Dr. Nevin Harner,[1] significant information was obtained on how youth between the ages of fifteen to twenty-four feel about adults who work with them in church organizations. In response to the question, "What three things about the adult who leads you do you like most?" were these answers:

Ability to understand and get along with young people, a splendid Christian character, interest in the things youth are interested in.

The three things they most object to are: being

bossed, being criticized too quickly, old-fashioned point of view.

They all agreed that they like enthusiasm in a leader and that the adult should know what she is trying to teach. They have no respect for one who does not.

It is a mistake to try to "put on" a program for Intermediates. They frankly say so if anybody is listening. They want the leader to work *with* them in expressing and putting into effect their *own* ideas. Adult leaders of this age can do their best work behind the scenes, suggesting, encouraging, even tactfully criticizing. The leader of youth in early adolescent years must be enthusiastic, stimulating, and intimate. In the later years she must be even less direct in her methods. Older young people need to be encouraged in freedom of thought and action rather than suppressed. If the leader takes to heart the things youth like and dislike about her leadership she will be accepted; otherwise she will find herself shut out though still present.

From the hour the baby is enrolled in the Sunbeam Nursery to the day that the young woman is promoted into the Woman's Missionary Society, there is one essential quality for all leaders. They must be liked by the young people they lead, in order to be successful. Never is there a time when this is not important. Statistics show that in industry and the armed forces morale is high and production good when human beings like and trust their leaders.

It is equally true in missionary organizations. If the children love their leader they will give her good behavior. If the adolescent likes the counselor the battle is two-thirds won.

But loving is a two-way street. Leaders have to love the children and young people in their organization. The younger the child, the harder he is to fool. Billie, three years old, replied to the over-dressed adult who insisted that the little girl sit in her lap, "No, I mess up your dress."

The leader may want to love the children but somehow does not quite make it. The children are rarely mistaken. The adolescent wants respect, not hand-holding, from the leader. They are no longer dependent children and they would like for the adult to know this too. The leader who without annoyance and irritation can work with the babies and young children who squirm and interrupt her and wander about and make noise; the older girls who whisper and giggle endlessly; the adolescents who speak with few inhibitions and walk roughshod over adult restraints, will surely have their admiration and confidence. "Love is the basis of learning," wrote Dr. Hymes. It is the beginning of missionary education for all youth, for "God is love."

### *Reasons for Too Few Leaders*

It is true that one cannot give something he does not possess. The plea for mission volunteers having met with meager response for many years reflects on the quality of leadership. This statement is not meant to discredit dedicated leaders of the missionary organizations in Southern Baptist churches. It is to point out that in many of our churches there exist conditions which contribute to the dearth of mission volunteers. These reasons are partially responsible for the lack of a sufficient number of counselors and leaders of youth organizations in Woman's Missionary Union.

In the first place, ignorance of where the denomination is at work and a lack of vision on the part of adults is a prime reason for failure to educate youth in missions. The command to "look on the fields" is ignored by the majority of Christians. They have taken precious little time to learn about the mission fields of their denomination. They read few, if any, books past or current which would enable them to know something of actual conditions in the countries that have been entered by Southern Baptists.

Many adults seldom see a mission magazine. "*The Commission?*" asked a YWA counselor with a rising inflection. "I honestly thought that was referring to Matthew 28:20." Some leaders rarely attend a convention or meeting where a missionary speaks. They have no vision of a world dying spiritually because two billions of people have rejected Christ or have not heard of him as their only hope of salvation. They give no evidence of deep concern for lost people whom they do not see or know.

The spirit of defeatism and a desire for security have been passed on to youth perhaps unconsciously but nonetheless, effectively. The adult says with a shrug:

> What's the use? The day of foreign missions is over. Doors are closed. Nobody can get into China; India is antimissionary; the Near East is equally disinterested; Catholics are not so bad. The gospel has gotten around into most of the corners of the globe. It is too great a risk anyway with all the nations of the world in revolt; with Russia and the United States in the greatest armament race in history.

Evangelical bodies in the United States and Canada are still trailing the 1928 figure for mission volunteers. "He who observes the wind will not sow; and he who regards the clouds will not reap" (Eccles. 11:4 RSV).

Adults have lowered the spiritual standards in their everyday living. The love of the world and a desire for pleasure and ease have invaded the lives of church members. There is often little evidence of genuine devotion to Christ and less of the spirit of sacrifice and prayer which must characterize a church if missionary volunteers are to come from its membership. Spiritual stamina is lacking where spiritual training has been superficial. Youth is not challenged by the undisciplined life led by many adults who pay lip service to the Christian way but walk in the broad path of the world. "Pretty mothers" need more equipment to lead youth into paths of service than knowing how to dispense tea with grace or dress in high fashion. These are only attractive accessories.

Liberal teaching in many churches has undermined faith in the Bible as God's revelation to man regarding sin and salvation. The result is that adults have lost confidence in the authority of the gospel and youth have followed after them. It is not true that one religion, including Christianity, is as good as another; that a composite of the well-known world religions is an answer to man's spiritual need.

It is well to remember that it was to the people who had the best religion known to the world that Christ first came. Centuries of following after religions in lands where they prevailed without competition before the advent of Christianity, did not give man a conception of personal worth or inward peace. One does not have to believe that other religions are wholly bad, to be zealous for the spread of Christianity. It is impossible to challenge youth to hazard all for Christ unless the leader believes with certainty that Jesus is actually "the way, the truth, and the life" and that no man cometh to the Father except by way of the Son.

### *What Leaders Should Know About Missions*

What is the adult leader's idea of missions? Is it circumscribed by the words "home," "foreign," "state," "community"? Or is the concept embraced in the term world missions? The churches in overseas mission areas are now largely self-governing and the missionaries work under the national leaders. Churches in countries where governments are unfriendly to evangelicals and subjected to pressure are carrying on without the help of a missionary. The "field" is the whole world and its evangelization begins at home. Young people need to know that spreading the good news of salvation is "missions" and it is news wherever Christ is not known whether in the home, across the street, across the nation, or across the ocean.

There are challenging situations within reach of each church. Thousands of people from distant places are living in the United States temporarily and expect to return to their homes. Forty thousand of these are overseas students, most of whom will return to places of leadership in their own countries. These nationals are in our communities. "The best way to export an idea is to wrap it up in a person," said a scientist about the exchange of foreign students. There is no better way to send the gospel into another land than to wrap it up in these students.

Any conception of missions that is not worldwide, beginning at home, is narrow and unworthy of leaders of a WMU organization. There is no "foreign" place; there is no "foreign" man.

The adult leader needs to realize that Southern

Baptists are not the only evangelicals sending missionaries to other countries. There are Christian bodies in Europe and Canada as well as many evangelical groups in the United States that have large missions in Asia, Africa, and South America. There are also other Baptist groups that support missions. Men and women who have been born again through the experience of regeneration share in making the good news of the gospel known to people everywhere.

Wherever Christian groups preach the resurrected living Lord, men and women who turn to him find salvation and freedom from sin. "Christians hold the world together" is as true today as in the second century.

The youth in our WMU organization need to have a deeper appreciation for the ministry of others who share the common task in carrying out the Great Commission. It is possible that some community missions projects could be more effectively developed if others like-minded and interested were enlisted.

The leader needs to know that important changes taking place on mission fields here and overseas are due largely to the success of the missionary enterprise of the nineteenth century. The story of Carey may not be familiar to every counselor or to all members of the organization she leads. It is a thrilling story and the beginning of an era when pioneer missionaries carried the gospel to the remote corners of the earth. They showed the way of salvation to millions of people. They built schools, hospitals, publishing houses, churches. Languages were reduced to writing, the Bible translated and made available to millions. They trained Christians whom they had won to be ready when the time came to assume leadership responsibilities. They planted the seed in good soil and today it is bearing a rich harvest in able national leadership both in churches and in government. These were men and women of great faith and courage who, like Carey, also expected great things from God and attempted great things for God.

The leader of youth needs to know, too, that the foreign mission movement in this country owes its beginning to the *youth* of America. Here again is a familiar story, but every leader and all members of Girls' Auxiliary and Young Woman's Auxiliary may not know it.

It was a group of young men from Williams College who held the famous Haystack prayer meeting while they were taking shelter from a storm. Here they pledged themselves to pray and work for the cause of foreign missions. Closely linked with the "Haystack" group are seven young men from different colleges who came together at Andover Theological Seminary to forge their mutual concern for missions.

As the memorial boulder in the "Missionary Woods" of Andover states, Adoniram Judson, Samuel Nott, Samuel J. Mills, Samuel Newell, Gordon Hall,

James Richards and Luther Rice by their "consecrated purpose to carry the gospel to the heathen world, led to the formation of the first American Society for Foreign Missions." This organization which came into being on May 18, 1814 in Philadelphia later was known as the Triennial Convention because it met every three years. The Baptist Third Jubilee Commemoration of 1964 is the anniversary of this event.

The magnetic personality of the tall, handsome Rice with the melodious voice and deep spiritual power was largely responsible for the organization of Baptists in America. His story—"The Man on the Horse"—is enough to make every youth, young man and young woman, feel the challenge of a great adventure that does not call them to a "life of slippered ease" but to hazard all for a cause bigger and grander than they.

*Leaders Must Communicate*

Adults must be willing to listen. Communication is a two-way traffic: person to person. If it is not two-way it is not complete communication. What does the baby have to say? the child? the Junior girl? the adolescent? Listen. How can this two-wayness be incorporated into missionary education tools such as the printed page, a film, a play or a story? The page, the speaker, the teacher must provide learning situations which appeal to the needs of the group; must get the same emotional effect as person-to-person communication. It is this quality which makes a mission study class a success. Programs from *The Window, Sunbeam Activities,* and *Tell* are merely recitations unless there is person-to-person communication. It is equally true in a play or a film. Good missionary dramas—whether projected or nonprojected—draw actors and audience into life situations that become personal completely apart from class, race, or nation.

Where does communication begin? It begins with the mother and her baby. If the Nursery leader, the GA and YWA counselors are successful they will keep on making the contact personal: leader to youth and youth to leader. Whatever the adult does in relationship to the youth whom she leads, she must make her contribution person to person. Somebody will listen, and then it is that young person's time to communicate her ideas and feelings.

Communication in missionary education for youth must be largely visual. One must remember the short attention span of the child, the inability of Juniors to concentrate for any length of time, the restlessness of the adolescent, the difficulty in catching the interest of more mature youth.

Scientific tests have proved the effectiveness of projected pictures as a teaching aid. The public school systems are making extended use of this medium in daily classroom work. The army uses projected pictures in training recruits.

The sight of a projector and a screen set up in the place of meeting has changed many a listless Intermediate GA and YWA member into an eager, expectant youth. Noisy Juniors become quiet when the lights are lowered and the first picture appears on the screen.

Not only can life on a mission field be depicted on the screen but so can many other phases of missions. Through filmstrips and slide sets children learn to appreciate "the happy differences" in people; they see what their gifts make possible through the Lottie Moon Christmas Offering and Annie Armstrong Offering; they learn steps to take in witnessing to an unsaved friend; how one person carries alone all the missionary work of Southern Baptists for a number of minutes each year.

These aids are not to be used for entertainment purposes but are always to be connected with what is going on and should be followed up with appropriate discussion.

Leaders need to be reminded that not all visuals are projected. Older Juniors and Intermediates can learn the geography of a mission field while they are engaged in making a relief map of the country. They can learn about the Cooperative Program dollar as they build it, segment by segment on a poster. They learn the history of any mission or institution on a mission field within a given period by making a time-line out of squares of cardboard strung on a cord, illustrated with pictures and carrying a few facts. Superb maps are available from many sources, but it is well to remember that Juniors like to and can make their own maps. The discussion or "talk" that follows the use of visuals will reveal to the leader whether or not communication has been two-way.

Adults must be able to impart missionary information in such a way that there will be action. Dr. Gerald Winfield, a director of mass communication in the countries where our government has technical assistance programs expressed the idea this way: "If the people don't buy your soap you are wasting your advertising." He relates an experience when he was a professor in a medical school in China. One of their projects was to promote basic sanitation among the Chinese villagers. The teams went into small towns with flip-charts, posters, and "a lot of talk." The people were eager to learn and they learned fast. They seemed to grasp and appreciate that the new health measures would revolutionize their lives for the better. They also took pride in their learning. It gave them a smug feeling of superiority. But they put away all these ideas in a compartment of the brain called "learning" and went on living exactly as they had always lived. The Chinese did not buy the soap. "We had wasted our time. We had not hit the responsive chord in their emotional nature that leads to action," for they had not *felt the need* to change their ways.

Communicating ideas is neither simple nor easy.

This is why leaders need to know children and young people and try to look into their hearts and minds. Ask them what they think about the use of money, or about the children of other nationalities in their school, about the film they have seen, the story to which they have just listened, or the book which they have studied, and they may give the answer that they think the leader expects. But listen to their remarks about people whether they live near or far. Was there any noticeable difference in attitude? Was there evidence of increase in gifts to missions or did the usual dime go into the church envelope when the allowance was $2.50? Did the YWA member who spoke well and fluently on the pending Lottie Moon Christmas Offering give no more than she did last year though she had had a substantial raise in salary? Was there more witnessing to the lost? More visitation?

One of two things is true. The leader either communicated her attitude which was not in harmony with her words or practice, or what she had tried to communicate had not stirred to action, the youth with whom she worked.

It is often no easier to communicate with God than with man. Here again we need to remember that real communication is two-way and person to person. The Christian leader must have had a personal encounter with Christ and must renew the contact daily in order to communicate God's redemptive purpose for all people.

*Qualities of Leadership*

So much depends on leadership in any part of missionary education. There are at least four characteristics that should mark a leader who undertakes to guide youth in this vital program.

First, a leader must have an undivided mind. There are many cultural and civic organizations which bid for the talents of adults. There is nothing wrong with these clubs except that they absorb a woman's time. She is torn between loyalty to the youth organization she has agreed to lead or counsel and the civic club in which she has accepted an office or committee chairmanship. Wavering between two responsibilities leads to a divided mind and this condition spells tragedy. The Bible so affirms.

Reread the story of Lot's wife. This woman was punished *by* her sin of backward-looking rather than for her sin. It reflected a state of mind that had tagged her since the day Lot pitched his tent toward Sodom. "No man can serve two masters," said Jesus. To the young man who came to him saying, "Lord, I will follow thee whithersoever thou goest," Jesus replied, "Foxes have holes, and the birds of the air have nests; but the Son of man hath not where to lay his head." By this he meant that he was as free of encumbrances as these forest creatures; that he was independent of distractions. So the leader cannot serve God and also follow after diverse things.

Many women are willing to accept positions of leadership on their own terms. Dabbling here and there in this activity and that means loss of power in service. One must be undivided in interest, time, strength, and will to find the highest joy in the work of the Lord. "This one thing I do," says the ordinary woman who can do the impossible with God's help if she is a woman of one purpose.

In the second place the leader must recognize that every young person has possibilities. Jesus had confidence in even the most unlikely human being; he saw in them a capacity for spiritual growth. Luther Burbank said that "Every weed is a possible flower." He was sure that the sour dock is not sweet because nobody had taken time to look to its possibilities. He was equally sure that the burweed would hold flowers instead of cockleburs on its stem if someone had taken trouble to look into a few principles of botany.

The child in perpetual motion; the inattentive, giggling Junior; the Intermediate, already air-borne, dreaming of the future and apparently indifferent to the leader's words; the cool young woman who is comparing her counselor's hairdo with the latest style—these young people are the future doctors, lawyers, teachers, scientists, preachers, and missionaries. Some of these young people, will stand before the mission boards of the Southern Baptist Convention and say, "God spoke to me when I was in a Sunbeam Band." "While I worked on Forward Steps in Girls' Auxiliary." "When I was a member of Young Woman's Auxiliary."

Judge Knox of the United States District Court, New York believed that "The life of almost any individual is apt to be the result of what catches his attention and fires his imagination in his youth." After knowing James Chalmers, pioneer missionary to the South Sea Islands, Robert Louis Stevenson exclaimed, "O Tamate, how different my life would have been had I known you in my youth!"

With patience, skill, and love, leaders in Woman's Missionary Union organizations can kindle in the hearts of the youth they lead, high appreciation for great souls who have lived nobly for Christ. The youth are beginning to carve out in their own minds careers for themselves. Despite all discouragements in outward behavior, leaders dare not minimize the opportunities before them to develop these potentialities of youth into vocations for Christian missions.

Thirdly, let the leader live in expectation. Today the organization meets. The leader does not anticipate anything out of the ordinary. She approaches the meeting in routine fashion. She expects the usual "faithful few." She may do this unconsciously so that she will not be disappointed. Hope is not in everybody's vocabulary. It is dangerous to prepare for and go to a missionary meeting in an expectant mood, but it is more dangerous if one does not.

There is value for leadership in living expectantly. So much depends on a leader's enthusiasm. Without it her leadership is dull and uninspired. With it life itself becomes interesting and vastly more worthwhile. Look at the cynic in Ecclesiastes. He had wealth, power, position, a discerning mind, but he lived under overcast skies because he had lost his zest for life. His philosophy is summed up in these bitter words, "Vanity of vanities, all is vanity and vexation of spirit." Paul is an example of the person who lives in the light of great expectation. Jails, stonings, shipwrecks, disappointment in people did not dim the brightness of his purpose to discover people for Christ.

Great discoveries in both the physical and spiritual realms have been made by men and women who lived in a state of expectancy. Other men had watched apples fall off trees, but it was Newton who discovered the law of gravitation. Many a lad had seen steam raise the lid of a teakettle, but Fulton envisioned this power to move a boat. Among the people who saw Jesus when he was cradled in a manger and later as a lad at the carpenter's bench, only a handful of shepherds, saintly Simeon, the woman, Anna, and a few Wise Men recognized him. They knew who he was because they were looking for him.

So it is with the leader who comes to the meeting in a state of expectancy. The room is in readiness, materials are out, every preparation that is possible has been made. The leader has not only mastered facts with imagination but she is aware of the necessity to hear, understand, and respect every person in the group. She waits with a prayer in her heart. This may be the day that Mary finds the emotional climate she needs which will lead her to discover life's real purpose.

Fourthly, the leader needs to accept her environment as a trust from God. Horace Bushnell expressed the idea in these words: "Bring your soul up to God to receive his work for you to do in your sphere, in your environment, under your cloud of obscurity, against your temptations, and then you shall find that your condition is never opposed to your good."

Bunyan's prison proved to be a palace for great thoughts. Kagawa's six-foot-square room in the slums of Tokyo brought more blessings to needy humanity than the most imposing mansion in a fashionable quarter of the city. The shabby streetcar on which the greathearted Laubach prayed, "just swishing God's love all around over the car," as he expressed it, became a place of worship as holy as the most imposing church. Rose Naranjo's kitchen took on the sanctity of a house of worship when she made plain the way of salvation to the women of her pueblo who had gathered to see the new electric washing machine.

A leader may not have an automobile, or a large house, or a telephone. She may have the handicap of an indifferent husband or a nagging relative who lives in her home. She may be married to a high-salaried executive, live in a handsome home, be required to entertain often and lavishly. Or she may be plagued by personal characteristics which ordinarily make leadership difficult. But if she has received her work from God she will discover that all these conditions are never opposed to her real success.

Are you able? When Salome asked Jesus to grant places of distinction in his kingdom to her two sons, James and John, he replied, "Ye know not what ye ask." Salome was an intelligent woman, no doubt, but her conception of living abundantly was rooted in position.

There are women in Woman's Missionary Union who are snared into leadership by the offer of a position or office. Nominating committees are as foolish as Salome when they attempt to flatter a woman into a place of responsibility.

When Salome asked that her sons might share the throne of Jesus, she failed to consider how he had won that place of power. He was coming into power through suffering on a cross. And he asked the simple question, "Are ye able to drink of the cup that I shall drink of?" With hardly a pause they quickly answered, "We are able." These were the men who later fell asleep in the Garden of Gethsemane while their Master agonized in prayer. These were the men who fled in that dark hour when the Roman soldiers took him away to be crucified.

Salome did not take into consideration the fitness of James and John for the position of eminence. God can give only what a person is ready to receive. He cannot do otherwise. It is useless for a leader to ask God to make her a success if she is unwilling to meet the requirements.

And the chief requirement?

Jesus said, "Whoever would be great among you must be your servant." Self-giving is the pathway to successful leadership. There are no short cuts—only a straight path. Are you able to walk in it?

4

# Youth in Woman's Missionary Union

From the beginning Woman's Missionary Union has had at its center the training of young people in the way of missions. The youth organizations are a vital part and "not an appendage." The Aims for Advancement set forth this purpose: It is to cultivate missionary convictions in the hearts of youth through:

Securing the co-operation of parents in the missionary education of their children
Maintaining a graded program of missionary education for youth
Adequate fostering of the WMU youth organizations of the church

The aim of all missionary education is to cultivate in children, young people, and adults a Christlike concern for people of every class, race, and nation; to know where and by what means we are proclaiming the gospel at home and abroad; to gain the participation of these children, young people, and adults in the work of spreading the gospel until it covers the earth (adaptation of Harner and Baker's definition).

The spirit of this aim is wrapped up in the word "beyond." Each person, child or adult, must be led to see beyond herself, her organization, and the activities in which all are engaged to the purpose of God that all mankind might come to know him through a personal knowledge of Christ as Saviour. Making Christ known is the missionary obligation of every Christian. It originated with God and not with man.

### Missionary Education Begins in the Home

It was said of frail Alice James, sister of the famous brothers Henry and William, that "she never accepted the horizon of invalidism." Neither does a home have to accept a narrow horizon of four walls. It is a farce for a self-centered person to claim Christlike concern for the peoples of the world; it is equally true of a family whose concerns do not reach beyond family-related interests.

Woman's Missionary Union believes and teaches that missionary education should begin in the home. No one can estimate the influence that parents have exerted in arousing and developing right attitudes and missionary interest on the part of their children. Little children absorb the negative feelings of their mothers in particular. The flash of an eye, a shrug of the shoulder, the tone of the voice, a spirit of indifference are caught long before the child can understand the words. The reverse is also true. What children hear their parents say about the preacher, the church, giving of money, missions, and missionaries colors their thinking all through life. The deposit, whether negative or positive, has been made in their minds and hearts and will remain.

The world was a small place in the days of our mothers and grandparents in a way quite different from the small world of today. The home and community were the "country," with father and mother king and queen; the relatives, such as cousins, uncles, and aunts, were the distant subjects who came to visit occasionally. In this little world children felt a measure of security.

With today's children, this has all changed. They talk glibly about Japan, Germany, Korea, Russia as if the countries were around the corner of the block or in the next community. Many fathers knew active duty in war in Europe, Asia, and later in Korea. Others have recently served their "time" in one of the armed services. Parents in large numbers are in colleges and seminaries in every section of the United States. Children have both the advantage and disadvantage of exposure to different ideas and living arrangements.

Television, radio, and the highly illustrated magazines and books have brought people and countries from distant places into the homes. Youth hear and are influenced by conversations and discussions over the air which reflect prejudice, immorality, and plain ignorance. These foes of Christian faith and decency can be countered by the instruction and conduct of parents. It is in the home that youth learns to appreciate people for what they are and not by what they have, where they live, or the color of their skin. The opposite is likewise learned in the home, too. There, youth can learn that all over the world are other Christian families who worship the same God and pray to the same Heavenly Father whom their families petition. The only difference is the language and possibly the posture—all insignificant differences. Parents can open the windows of the home so that their children will look out on the world with awareness and understanding.

For the young child, the atmosphere of the home in which he grows for the first few years will have great bearing on his future attitude toward people and God. This is the place where his missionary education begins. In a happy home where love and sharing are demonstrated, leaders and counselors of youth have a foundation on which to build future concepts of God's love for a lost world.

Children's ideas about the people of other races, creeds, and nations stem from the home and are fixed by the time they are six. Rodgers and Hammerstein[1] said it in *South Pacific:*

You've got to be taught before it's too late
Before you are six or seven or eight,
To hate all the people your relatives hate
You've got to be carefully taught!

## How the Home Helps Undergird Missionary Education

G. K. Chesterton once wrote, "Nothing is real until it becomes local." Christian concern can become local first in the home. This is another way of saying that one cannot in reality be very much concerned about what is taking place across the nation or ocean until an interest is shown in what is happening nearer at hand.

*Conversation at the table* can be used to gain information, to reveal attitudes, and to correct wrong ideas.

"Oh, boy, my favorite food!" shouted David. "Teri-yaki and rice! Let me at it."

"You rice eater," said Linda, the sister. "We'll send you back to China."

"Japan," corrected David. "Teri-yaki is Japanese."

"Why do Chinese and Japanese always eat rice? Don't they get tired of it?" continued Linda.

"It's like our bread," their mother replied. "You eat bread every meal and you don't get tired of it."

"That's right," Linda agreed. "I hadn't thought about that. But why do we have bread and Chinese have rice?" she continued.

Her father took this one, "Because bread is usually made of wheat and wheat doesn't grow in Japan or China or most of Asia. Rice grows there in the rainy low valleys and the people eat what grows best."[2]

On another evening the table talk went something like this:

"Cookie and I were Chinese dolls today," announced Carol, who was in nursery school.

"How were you Chinese dolls?" asked Linda.

"We wore long dresses made like Miss Wai's," explained Carol. "Teacher combed my hair with bangs, but Cookie's hair wouldn't make bangs." The child added, "Cookie and I are sisters."

"Sisters?" Linda was puzzled.

"Yes, teacher said God was the Father of us all and that makes us sisters."

The sympathetic father added, "It is true, Carol, that God made us all and loves every one of us. Some day when you are older you will understand that we become his children in a special way."

He was too wise a father to attempt a further explanation of the difference between being a child of God by creation and his child through the new birth.

*Books and missionary stories* have always played a significant part in extending horizons and influencing the lives of youth. A love for reading usually begins in the home. There is no such thing as a born reluctant reader. Something has happened to a young person to create this state of mind. It usually can be traced to his home.

Children and older young people are stirred by the stories and experiences of pioneer missionaries. Lottie Moon never got away from *The Lives of the Three Mrs. Judsons.* Carey, plying his shoemaker's trade, was influenced by the story of David Brainerd and his work among the Indians of North America. The adolescent is in the hero-worship period. The *Heroes of the Cross* series put the stories of great mission areas within easy reach of every boy and girl. The home is the best place to introduce youth to the real heroism that these men and women displayed in taking the gospel across geographic frontiers of the world.

Southern Baptists have produced their own series of modern-day heroes under the titles of *More Than Conquerors, Much to Dare,* and *A Path of Light.* Woman's Missionary Union has published the *King's Way Series.* All three series include stories of both home and foreign missionaries.

Parents who surround their children with the kind of books they want them to read will have their act of anticipation well rewarded. In the meantime the child may be waiting to have his taste whetted for books by hearing Bible and missionary stories read to him. Older young people find reading aloud in the family circle pleasant and frequently discussion-provoking. *The World in Books* catalog and the *YWA Book Club List* are sources from which to draw books most likely to stimulate a missionary interest among youth.

Many great missionaries of earlier days received first impressions for Christian service, in the home. Alexander Mackay's mother told him missionary stories and he watched his father trace on a map of Africa the journeys of David Livingstone. The prayers of John G. Paton's father and mother sent him to the New Hebrides. David Livingstone received his first missionary impressions from his father's missionary stories. Many former and present leaders in the organizations of Woman's Missionary Union are in service because of the missionary atmosphere of their homes.

An excellent example of capitalizing on a happy family incident to stimulate reading is told by Mary Norfleet in *The World from Our Home.* Her nine- and seven-year-old boys attended a birthday party given by a young friend whose grandmother had sent to the children a *piñata* from Mexico. It was made of pink tissue paper in the form of a bull's head, and was filled with toys and candy. When the Norfleet children came home all they could talk about was the fun they had breaking the *piñata* and scrambling for the goodies. They were ready to like Mexico and Mexicans. Their mother enriched this experience by having them read together "A *Piñata* for Pepita," from *Told Under the Stars and Stripes,* anthology of stories about American children of varied cultural backgrounds.

*Family worship* can be a time when the missionaries on the calendar of prayer are remembered. Parents know about the prayer calendar through their children and young people who are in Girls' Auxiliary and Young Woman's Auxiliary. In *Tell* and *The Window,* the names of both home and foreign missionaries are listed on their birthdays. The chosen verse for the day, coupled with a brief missionary story taken from *Royal Service* which usually carries a prayer request, provides the whole family with a worship experience that is definitely linked with the missionary work of the denomination. Here is also an opportunity to share with the family any personal item about the missionary whom a child in Sunbeam Band, the daughters in GA or YWA may know.

Jane had returned from the YWA conference at Ridgecrest. There she had met and heard several missionaries. When their names appeared on the prayer calendar in *The Window* she never failed to relate at the breakfast table bits of biography or information about their work. The family looked forward to this brief but happy time together when all their horizons were being expanded because a member was a part of Woman's Missionary Union. Later the father confessed that he had become intensely interested in the separation of church and state primarily because his daughter had related with vividness the lack of religious freedom in Spain which she had learned about from the missionaries at Ridgecrest. He had carried over the truth into the home arena. And it all had its beginning at family prayers.

"The Whole Family Tithing" is the title of a leaflet published by Woman's Missionary Union. Parents should discuss the church budget with their children and explain how the money is used. By setting the example of tithing and encouraging their children to do likewise they undergird the cause of missions and follow up the training given to their children in the youth organizations of Woman's Missionary Union. A cherished memory of one woman in WMU goes back to her youth when the father gave to this young daughter a portion of the tithe, and together father, mother, and child prepared envelopes for Sunday's service. Then the father prayed that the money would be used to preach the "blessed Word to the heathen in darkness." She has never been able to get away from that home example and worship experience in giving.

*Family tours to mission fields* open up whole new areas to every member. Increased missionary fervor has been noticeable in those who have taken advantage of the opportunities to see home missions firsthand in the Southwest. Every year more families go to WMU conferences. One father said he had "come along with his wife to keep the boys from underfoot." Then he confessed that all of them had gone to hear a missionary every day, were in each evening service, and had visited every Spanish and

Indian mission within fifty miles of Glorieta Baptist Assembly.

A further contribution of the home in creating a missionary interest as a background for missionary education in the church is *entertaining overseas students and guests from abroad.* Nobody is quite the same who has sat down in her living room with a homesick person from another country, listened to the falteringly told story about distant home and family, looked at pictures of parents, brothers and sisters, and heard stumbling English words that spoke plainly of loneliness and a desire to be loved and understood. That country will never again be just a political uncertainty in the world's scramble for friends, or a colored spot on a map, for the young visitor has provided a living bond with this particular land. So it goes when nationals come into our homes. They make the program of missionary education live.

There are other ways in which missionary education can be made real in the home: *use of dolls, maps, and music* are further examples. Dolls of other lands are "but models of people." Children in the home learn about the dress and customs through this intriguing hobby. Mickey, age three, received from her grandmother a pair of Hong Kong handmade dolls. Her mother explained that these were Chinese dolls and that they were made by Christians who learned about Jesus from the missionaries. After a bit of talk which included appropriate Chinese names, the little girl ran off to her room with the new treasures. Several hours later the mother writing to the grandmother asked Mickey if she had any message to send. There was a moment's silence, then, "Ask Gran if Birmingham is in the United States." Already she was beginning the study of geography against a missionary background.

Every home can afford some kind of a map or globe. In one home a large world map is fastened on the wall of a Primary-age girl's room. It is placed low enough that she can follow the route of any member of the family who is traveling to mission points. She has acquired interesting bits of information which she proudly shares with the members of her Sunbeam Band.

Through *singing and playing the music of other countries,* it is possible to give youth in the home an appreciation of these cultures.

There are many songbooks that contain songs of every type sung by the children in almost every land. *The Whole World Singing* and *Missionary Melodies* are two of such books. It is fun to try these songs when overseas guests or missionaries are visiting in the home. To hear words in a different language sung in a familiar melody is an exciting adventure for both young people and adults. When these international visitors are Christians and the song is a hymn, everybody is moved with a new emotion of worldwide Christian fellowship. Members of the family come to appreciate the music of composers of different nationalities through excellent recordings.

A father and mother and two little girls four and six were traveling by car on a vacation trip. "Mother!" Pam exclaimed. "Where is our hymn book?" Mother had failed to put it in, but they all knew so many hymns they did not really need a book. First one child, then the other started a hymn and mother and dad joined in. Pam and Nancy knew all the stanzas to each hymn. Some of their favorites were "Jesus Loves the Little Children of the World," "I Love to Tell the Story," and "The Star-Spangled Banner." They had the words in their hearts though the full meaning would grow through the years.

Christmas provides an opportunity for the family to sing together those carols which are representative of different countries. The occasion will have greater meaning if one of the girls who is in GA or YWA is asked to tell the origin of the carol and how Christmas is celebrated in that land. Excellent choral groups have made recordings of carols, but the greatest value comes when the family makes its own music.

Woman's Missionary Union further stresses parent interest in the missionary education of their children through *child-parent meetings at the church* when some special mission activity is under way and through *home visitation by counselors and leaders.* Through these various means Woman's Missionary Union seeks to plant in the hearts of parents worldwide concern for people who do not know God.

**Graded Program for Missionary Education of Youth**

The graded program of Woman's Missionary Union includes Sunbeam Band, Girls' Auxiliary, Young Woman's Auxiliary and, until 1953, The Order of Royal Ambassadors which is now under the direction of the Baptist Brotherhood.

*Sunbeam Band*

The fiftieth anniversary of the organization of Sunbeam Band was held in St. Louis in 1936. Seated on the platform surrounded by children and young people was Dr. George Braxton Taylor, the "Cousin George" who helped Mrs. Anna Folsom in Fairmont (Virginia) church organize the first Sunbeam Band. It was a memorable occasion when Dr. Taylor addressed the convention. Prophetic of the future growth and development of this organization and the extent of its influence were these words, "If we may multiply by tens of thousands our Sunbeams, we will multiply year by year in untold numbers church members who know about world needs, about the transforming power of the gospel, who have formed the habit of glad, generous, regular gifts for preaching the saving grace of God to earth's remotest bound."[3]

Woman's Missionary Union believes these words so strongly that it has developed a missionary program for children in Southern Baptist churches beginning at birth and extending through eight years of age. Odd as it may seem in this day of graded missionary organizations, young people of all ages were included in the Sunbeam Band in those early days. With the passing of time separate organizations were formed: Young Woman's Auxiliary in 1907, the Order of Royal Ambassadors in 1908, and Girls' Auxiliary in 1913. It was not until 1956 that Woman's Missionary Union voted to divide the Sunbeam Band in two age levels, Beginner Sunbeam Bands (ages 4 and 5) and Primary Sunbeam Bands (ages 6 through 8), though for many years prior to this date the Plan of Work had suggested the two groups.

Still moved by the prophecy of Dr. Taylor, which had been made current by a real need, the Union voted in 1957 to include the babies in its organized work of missionary education.

Mothers were bringing their three-year-olds to Beginner Sunbeam Band. Leaders found an impossible situation on their hands. These toddlers were too young to do the Beginner work, yet the mothers wanted to attend the meetings of the Missionary Society. Out of this growing need came the Sunbeam Nursery. The purpose of the new organization is to provide suitable learning experiences for children, birth through three, while mothers are attending the Woman's Missionary Society meetings.

In a previous chapter the characteristics of these babies and young children are pointed out. They cannot be overlooked if the leader expects to train the instinctive impulses into ways that will lead the child to God and to a knowledge of his purpose for the redemption of the world. Effectively and in keeping with the best-known laws of learning, the plan for the missionary education of these children from birth through three are set forth and developed in units of study in the Sunbeam Nursery.

The co-operation of the mother is vital to the success of this nursery program. The leader must work in close contact with her. Every mother needs to feel that her child is, above all, safe; that she will be called if she is needed; that she can trust the leader and be willing to share the child's love with her. If leader and mother do not like each other, nothing can be done with the child. Love is the key word at the beginning stage, in the missionary education of the young child.

The fours and fives are beginning to learn about others outside the home. Their characteristics have been dealt with also in a previous chapter, but it is well to call attention to the fact that at this age a child can form a better concept of God who loves all children. He soon learns that by helping others and sharing what he has with the children in his group that he is expressing God's love and care for all. At this age he can learn to have a wholesome attitude toward all children regardless of where they live or what they have or how much they know or what is the color of their skin. He can pray in his own words, thanking God for the wonders of nature, his friends, and his home. As he learns about children in other places he can easily be led into praying for them. With patience and skill the leader of the four- and five-year-olds will help them to realize that all children do not know that God loves them. This is the major emphasis; therefore, it is essential that they have pleasant experiences in their church, guided by friendly leaders.

With the coming of the school age, life of the Primary child turns a corner. This event means enlarged environment with new friends, new sources of information, new interests in a larger world, and new problems for the leader. Atmosphere and attitudes have been the major concern of the leader up to this point. She has been laying the foundation of sharing and helpfulness; consideration and respect for others; trusting God as a loving Father.

Now her chief concern is to strengthen these attitudes by action. This does not mean that previous efforts have been periods of inactivity. Nothing could be farther from the actual truth. It means that the older child can see and understand for himself some of the needs of others, some of the activities of his church, and that the greatest thing he has to share with others is God's love.

The successful leader takes conscious recognition of the child's traits at this stage of his development. Though differences in people of other races must be recognized, accepted, and appreciated for the contributions they have made to our own culture, more and more emphasis should be placed on the similarity of children everywhere. Whatever techniques are used, children in Sunbeam Bands should be led to see that basic needs are the same for all people. Everybody needs food, some kind of clothes, a house to live in, a school to attend, work to do, the love and security of a family, and God to worship. The series called *Around the World Picture Books* by Millen and Smalley are true-to-life sketches about children's homes, pets, toys, games, and ways of worship in other lands. Had the fathers and mothers of this generation, when they were of Primary age, known more about children in other parts of the world, World War II might not have occurred.

The units of study for Beginner and Primary Sunbeam Bands are in *Sunbeam Activities*, the quarterly magazine since 1953 for leaders of Sunbeam Bands.

For several years Woman's Missionary Union felt the need to strengthen the work for the eight-year-olds. In 1959 extra features were provided for this age. They include a special name, "World Friends," and a children's booklet in which permanent activities are set forth in sections with space provided for parents to check when the child has completed a given section. This in nowise is to take the place of the Primary Units of study in *Sunbeam Activities*. These continue to be the basis of the eight-year-olds' missionary education.

As a further aid to strengthening the eight-year-old program a day camping plan has been developed. This is an attractive and worthwhile activity to stimulate increased interest in missions. In the leaflet, "Day Camping for 8-year-old Sunbeam Bands," leaders will find adequate directions for a successful day camping experience.

Training of children in world friendship is the responsibility of Woman's Missionary Union. This high missionary purpose cannot be achieved by teaching a child to "say" Scripture verses or recite glibly facts about mission stations, goals for mission offerings, or conditions on mission fields. It is important to recall that a child learns 10 per cent of what he hears, 50 per cent of what he sees, and 90 per cent of what he does.

In her book *Missionary Education of Beginners,* Jessie Moore[4] says:

"We put our young people into a laboratory to learn chemistry, the playground to learn baseball, but we seat our children each in his own chair to learn the Golden Rule and are satisfied when it is recited letter perfect. We send them to a table to color a picture of a charming Japanese maid and think we are training them in missions while two of those children are fussing over the red crayon."

Basic training in world friendship begins with that red crayon!

*More thoughts for leaders.* More than a superficial knowledge of the Bible is necessary for the leader of children in Sunbeam Bands. The Bible is a missionary book. Without a Bible-based conviction that man is completely lost and that spiritually he can be found only through God's universal love, the teaching will be at its best merely humanitarian. Human need will take precedence over divine imperative. The leader should not teach the child things about God that he will have to unlearn when he is older. He should receive answers to his questions at the level of his understanding. He needs to learn that God loves him and loves all children; that wrong can be forgiven.

The leader's reading should be as broad as time and money will allow. At the same time she should be familiar with a few good books dealing with children of this age. In preparing to use a unit of study in *Sunbeam Activities* the leader should "read herself full."

There are always suggested books in the magazine which will enrich the learning experiences of the children. Travel agencies and the information service of a country are excellent sources for background materials. The latter can be obtained through a nation's embassy in Washington. Often posters and booklets may be secured.

There are times, however, when nothing seems to help. The leader does not know what to do with the material before her. There is *too much* for some; not enough for others. At this point she should take counsel with the organization purposes and remind herself that she is not teaching a *unit* but *children.* She can study *with* them and together they can travel the adventurous road in world friendship for Christ's sake.

*Young Woman's Auxiliary*

Scattered throughout the South, Baptist young women had their own mission societies prior to 1888 but they were not called Young Woman's Auxiliary until 1907. The missionary purpose is the same for youth as for children, the same for adults as for youth. The basic elements do not change. Only in degree of understanding and methods of implementing is there change.

Counselors of Young Woman's Auxiliary have not always recognized as basic the need of youth to have their own organization with their own officers and committees. The counselor may have set up a letter-perfect organization but the feeling of ownership by the young women is lacking. If this organization is to provide the proper climate for growing missionary-minded young women it will have to be theirs. The trait of leading from behind has already been discussed in chapter three. This does not mean that the counselor is not needed; but it does mean that the leadership needs to do more encouraging and counseling and less taking over of the real responsibility. Young Woman's Auxiliary can become the living heart of all the youth work in the church under sympathetic, intelligent, consecrated leadership.

Through more than fifty years of steady growth, Woman's Missionary Union has been looking at the young women sixteen through twenty-four who are in Southern Baptist churches. Experience has proved the wisdom of providing a separate organization for high school girls and another for the unmarried young business women under twenty-five.

There is no difference in the organizational structure. Aims for Advancement are the same. Experience, however, has again pointed out the fact that there are more girls enlisted in the High School YWA than in the Business YWA. Without going into all reasons for this difference, one of them could well be that with the latter group WMU leadership has not recognized that its task is to put young women to work. This is a part of the aim of missionary education, and participation by the members of the auxiliary is absolutely necessary and valuable. Issues at home and abroad need the energy and optimism of these young women at work on them. It is not enough to meet, sing, "give parts," visit a shut-in, eat, and go home. The missionary movement has always challenged youth to action!

*A fact-finding project.* Members of Young Woman's Auxiliary should not be robbed of this opportunity to tackle world problems on the local level. The study of any nationality in a program from *The Window* or in a current mission study book should find expression at home. In the first place the natural reaction should be to attempt a fact-finding project. Nationals from the country studied may not be nearby, but a look around in the community may reveal other people who need friendship and help. A project—and a project is nothing more than a purposeful activity—should grow out of the interests of the members themselves and represent what they want to do. This places a heavy responsibility on the leader, for if the right techniques are used these alert young women will want to take up a purposeful activity.

The story of the Great Lakes area as a mission field was stressed a few years ago during the Week of Prayer for Home Missions and later in May, 1960 issue of *The Window*. The thrilling account of building waterways, canals, and industries was vividly related. A natural reaction might have been "Who does the work in America?" The local missionary implication is obvious. Under imaginative leadership young women could quickly have seen the relationship close by. "Who works here in our town, our city, our community?" This should lead to exploring the working relations in factories and industries to the end that people without Christ are discovered and witnessed to. This type investigation is not a social science class type of project, though techniques learned in secondary schools will be extremely helpful. Many of the young women will have this kind of know-how and should be allowed to share their knowledge in making plans.

*Service projects* are a "natural" for the members

of Young Woman's Auxiliary. The need for World Relief is as great now as in the days immediately after World War II. Calls continue to come from overseas for clothes, shoes, food, bedding. The "Christmas tree in August" has found youth eager to bring gifts for many home mission fields. A service project of great popularity was providing supplies for the Baptist hospital in Nalerigu, Ghana, West Africa. A word of caution is advisable for it is easy to think of all service projects as "community missions." It is the latter only when the object of concern is within the bounds of the association.

An examination of home mission territory will show how great a number of mission points are within driving distance of many Baptist churches—*A mission tour* could be to a Good Will Center, an Indian church, a migrant camp, a kindergarten school, or to a whole field such as in French Louisiana or the Spanish mission in Pueblo, Colorado or Santa Fe, New Mexico or the Seminole work in Florida, or among the Choctaws in Mississippi and the Cherokees in North Carolina. There is no end to the possibilities. YWA members could arrange to spend an afternoon, or a day if possible, visiting a nearby mission area. Many needs will be readily seen and should be reported to the organization. Perhaps leadership needs for a club or a recreation program can be provided or some special activity that the missionary is planning can be met. Whatever the outcome, the tour will give young women a new insight into the work of their Home Mission Board and arouse in them a desire to do something about what they see.

High school and college students are being trained in school and by clubs to think about national and world affairs. They have studied the United Nations. To better understand its working they have set up a "UN" in school where mock General Assembly and Security Councils programs are put on. They have debated world issues. Whether Red China should be admitted was tackled by a senior high group with a barrage of facts both pro and con that revealed both knowledge and skill in debate. The moral issues were heavily underscored. A panel handled assistance to the race problem with insight and remarkable objectivity. Technical assistance offered by our government to the less developed countries of the world has been the topic for discussion and debates in many schoolrooms over the United States.

All of these subjects have missionary overtones. They should be made to contribute to the young woman's understanding of the effect those problems have on the work Southern Baptist missionaries attempt to do. Has the United States arbitrated a dispute in a country where Southern Baptists have work? This question can provoke a realistic study of the Middle East, with a map of the area as a working basis, and a close tie-in with the effect on the mission work in Gaza, Lebanon, Israel, and Jordan.

An understanding of the technical assistance program will show that once much of this type of work was done by the missionary. In the call for men and women to go out and help develop the land, educate the poor, and bring health to the sick, youth can see that here is an opportunity for a life commitment, whether as an employee of the government or as a missionary under the Foreign Mission Board. Both places provide an opportunity for them to witness in the name of Christ.

Another vital study project can be the Christian and race. Youth seems to be able to bring more objectivity to this problem than adults. It is a good thing to let the members of Young Woman's Auxiliary try their hands, hearts, and minds at it. No single world problem has had or is having greater bearing on the work of foreign missions than this disturbing issue. There are many sources of information for such a study to be found in books, daily newspapers, magazines both popular and missions, denominational periodicals, leaflets, and films. A study of this kind will eventually lead to action, the climax to all missionary education. An exchange of meetings between the YWA and the Red Circle Girls in a Negro church is a step in this direction. A new day will have arrived when high school and college YWAs take on a *study project* as a normal outgrowth of interest already aroused in world affairs.

Young women have a ready-made situation for these study projects in working on requirements for the YWA citation.

*Young women away from home.* Hundreds of the ablest young women around the age of eighteen annually leave their homes and churches and go to college and nursing school for four years or more. Here they may face ideas and ways of life that unsettle them. The ties with the home church are broken; they often do not find their way into the churches in the college community. So they "sit down between two chairs." The evidence is that church attendance falls off.

There are YWA organizations for these students to help them keep alive the missionary spirit. In schools of nursing the organization is called Grace McBride, and on college and university campuses it is called Ann Hasseltine. Special bulletins from the YWA department in Birmingham are sent regularly to the members of these organizations, and state YWA offices, also, should keep close contact with them.

A fact of significance to note is that the place where the first blow to religious faith comes has changed. It used to be in college; now it is in high school, according to selected studies made by authorities in the field of religious education. One survey of four hundred students showed that 69 per cent of them lost their belief in a personal God or immortality during the high school years. For this reason the church at home should undergird the young woman's faith before she packs her trunk for the college town. Active participation in Young Woman's Auxiliary in her own church will go a long way toward holding her steadfast. Her faith has been strengthened by a knowledge of the failure of other world religions to meet the basic spiritual needs of man. Christian truth will stand the searchlight of science, for truth is a unit. Difficulties arise when only a little corner of truth is regarded as the whole.

*YWA Conference.* No discussion of missionary education for YWAs should omit the Convention-wide YWA Camp. Beginning with the year 1960 the conference alternates between Glorieta, New Mexico, and Ridgecrest, North Carolina. Since 1923 young women of the Southern Baptist Convention have been coming together for study, inspiration, and recreation. The program is varied enough to suit all tastes. The call for mission volunteers has been responded to in ever-increasing strength of purpose. Few YWAs in the Convention have gone completely untouched by the influence of Ridgecrest and Glorieta conferences. The list of missionaries who made a life commitment during these weeks grows longer year by year. Other YWAs have attended state camps and houseparties where dedications to full-time Christian service have been made. The heart of missionary education is life commitment.

*Girls' Auxiliary*

"When girls grew too big for the Sunbeam Bands there were long years to wait before they were eligible for membership in Young Woman's Auxiliary," reports Mrs. W. J. Cox in *Following in His Train.* During this time the girls were more or less sponsored by the YWA and were called Junior Auxiliaries. In 1913 they were given a name, a hymn, a motto, and a manual of methods. From that time to the present Girls' Auxiliary for girls ages nine through fifteen has been the fastest growing organization in Woman's Missionary Union.

*Junior Girls' Auxiliary.* For many years Woman's Missionary Union recognized the wisdom of dividing the girls according to ages. Juniors were divided from Intermediates in recognition of the inability to hold the interest of the nine-year-old and the fifteen-year-old with the same type program and activities. Authorities on youth agree that the Intermediate is happiest with her own age and in a small group. Studies in adolescent psychology show that fourteen members is an average number among spontaneous neighborhood groups.

In the program of missionary education for Juniors there are several objectives to follow which are all related to the general aim of missionary education. This is the age when the greatest number of children accept Christ as Saviour. A leader must be deeply concerned if there is in her organization a single girl who is not a Christian. It is inconsistent with the total idea of missions to be less concerned about the child at home than those far away who are not Christians. In a way impossible to achieve with Sunbeam Band age children, these Junior GAs who have so recently been led to the Lord can understand that now they must help to carry the message of salvation to every part of the earth.

This is the age of curiosity, as was pointed out in chapter three. Girls in GA are interested in girls of other lands, the kind of homes they live in, the food they eat, the schools they attend, what kind of games they play, the clothes they wear. It is logical to begin with these natural interests and build on them through definite activities such as storytelling, dramatization, playing games, making murals, as the girls develop in Christian concern. Through activities which capitalize on the inherent traits of these young girls, interest and respect for the children in other lands are built up. Playing out missionary stories appeals to Juniors and is an excellent way to place in their hearts a desire to share with others.

*Tell,* the magazine for Girls' Auxiliary, and the mission study books in the graded series produced by the Home and Foreign Mission Boards show where mission work is carried on by Southern Baptists. Through the excellent program of Forward Steps, additional information about fields and missionaries is learned. Thousands of girls have felt the thrill of accomplishment and the burden of the world for Christ as they have climbed step by step until the day, as Intermediate GAs, they attained Queen Regent recognition. More than one missionary has publicly stated that she heard the call to the mission field as she worked on Forward Steps.

The Junior girl has a strong sense of ownership but she also likes to help. This natural impulse can be directed toward sharing what she has with those in need. Service projects can be a spiritual experience for the girls.

Mary Ann ran home, literally, to tell her mother the GAs were to gather clothes for a Korean family who lived in the town and were in distress. "I want you to let me have my Christmas dress to give," she said, quite out of breath.

"Your Christmas dress!" said the mother in astonishment, for she knew her ten-year-old daughter loved the red corduroy jumper and white blouse better than any dress she had. The color was the reason she called it her Christmas dress. "But why that dress? You have others just as good," tempted the mother.

"No, mother, I don't have any dress as good as my Christmas dress, for I love it most."

The dress found its way to the box that the GAs themselves helped to pack.

Missionary education for Juniors includes giving and praying. Giving, though a vital part of a Junior's spiritual development, needs to be directed toward people rather than causes. The little girl in the Primary Sunbeam Band has learned about God's ownership and that some of what she has belongs to him. When she is promoted to Girls' Auxiliary she meets the Cooperative Program, which may or may not be easy for her to grasp. This is why the words, if used, need to be spelled out in terms of people and what they need. Above all, the Junior must be trained to see that the tithe she puts into her church envelope and the gift she brings in her bank for the Lottie Moon Christmas Offering and the Annie Armstrong Offering are her part in sharing with the rest of the world.

If the child has not been given an allowance previously, when she becomes a Junior GA she should have a regular amount for which she is responsible. When she is old enough to earn money she should be encouraged to do so. Stewardship concepts are not likely to become deeply rooted until one learns how to earn, spend, save, and give. The Junior GA will need both guidance and example set by parents and counselors.

Juniors like to remember the missionaries by name on the prayer calendar. They are listed in *Tell* on their birthdays. The experience of prayer can be deep and meaningful to the girl who has been led step by step through all the stages of activity in her Auxiliary to recognize in her heart the purpose of what she has been learning while doing. It cannot be underscored too often that this responsibility lies with the leader.

*Intermediate Girls' Auxiliary.* Girls of this age

require activity in their program. They must at least be active in mind and voice. Chapter three points out that one of the strongest obvious traits these youth possess is their determination not to lean on adults. They lean heavily on one another, hence the closely knit gangs. True, the major missionary education objectives for Juniors are also for Intermediates as they are for all ages. They are expressed differently and developed in various ways. Leadership should work in closest harmony with these girls, keeping in mind the adolescent's impulse to create and her eagerness to do something well. "It is a wise leader who gets nature on her side in the missionary education of adolescents!"

Various phases of missionary education which relate to Intermediates have already been developed in this and previous chapters. Here again special attention is called to the value of projects. The girls should be given an opportunity to select an activity from a number of possibilities. Every program in *Tell* and every mission study book hold out possibilities which the members can discover for themselves. There may be and should be skilful guidance by the counselor but if the experience is to mean what lies within it, the counselor will allow the group to see and agree on the project.

Map-making of places where missionaries are, investigating a need or problem near at hand, pursuing hobbies such as stamp collecting, service projects, role-playing neighborhood relationships, inviting guests of minority groups for parties or teas, dramatizing the life of a missionary—all can lead from the interests of the group to better understanding of people and their needs. Once when a film was used in a program the counselor, through the program chairman, suggested that certain members watch specific characters. After the film some of the girls rewrote the episode or wrote new ones.

State camps and houseparties are ideal situations for group participation in the project-type activity. Here opportunities are given for individual expression in an emotional climate where the girl feels free to express herself. The informal atmosphere of camp can become a medium of sharing Christian love and concern, a channel for the Holy Spirit to work in the hearts of girls seeking God's purpose for their lives.

Training in giving can take on deeper meaning at this age. Out of the experiences of learning about people and life through projects, the plan of giving as developed by Southern Baptists can become a project within itself. Any single missionary program in *Tell* can serve to create a desire to know how the missionaries are supported and their work financed. This incentive may be used to investigate how the Cooperative Program works. In turn, attention can be given to the way the money they give is used in their own church. Giving, then, becomes personal and related to the needs they have felt and the desire to meet these needs.

In these ways Intermediates discover that they are a part of the world mission enterprise. As a result of their research they should be encouraged to share their findings with other groups in the church or a GA in another church. Giving of their money may be the nearest the majority of these Intermediates will ever get to the mission field.

What has been said about Juniors in relationship to prayer applies to Intermediates. Praying for the missionaries by name makes identification with them possible outside and beyond the limitations of space and time. Lifting facts to the Father and listening, with the willingness to follow, has led youth of every age to offer themselves for lifetime service in places of need.

**Fostering Youth Organizations**

Since the year 1896 when the Sunbeam Band was adopted by Woman's Missionary Union, the organization has sought to nurture the missionary spirit and the grace of giving in children, girls, and young women in Southern Baptist churches. This aim is inherent in the purpose of Woman's Missionary Union and today is achieved by fostering all WMU youth organizations in the church.

The concept of fostering has grown with the expansion of missionary opportunities and a deepening conviction that making known God's redemptive purpose is the chief concern of all Christians. To help the youth in our churches understand missions and their part in making Christ known to all the world can be best accomplished through organizations of their own.

Many ways of fostering have been advocated and put into practice. These means have run the gamut from nothing much more than physical exercise to work that involves genuine spiritual giving. Using the car to bring children to the place of meeting, serving refreshments, buying supplies for programs and books for study, providing magazine subscriptions for the organization are all good in their place. To stop with these material helps is to miss the point in fostering. The mother organization will have to look farther and deeper.

Providing leaders is the biggest and most challenging part in fostering. Over and over one hears the cry, "But where do you find them?" Dr. Carleton Mayer in his book, *Young People in Your Church,* relates an experience he had during a conference on youth work. A member of the group told in stirring language how his church had built up its program of work with young people. When he had finished speaking a preacher rose and said, "Brother, that's a great story and I can see how you did it with all those leaders. But what I want to ask is where do you get them?" Like a flash the young man replied, "Grow them!" This is the answer to the problem of leadership. No miracle. Just a careful job of leadership training.

Woman's Missionary Union has leadership training courses for every age group. The Woman's Missionary Society can do no greater fostering than to provide continuous training opportunities in missions for the leadership of Sunbeam Bands, Girls' Auxiliaries, and Young Woman's Auxiliaries.

The tide will turn. Instead of the cry of no trained leaders there will be dedicated women ready to step into places of responsibility as directors, counselors, and leaders of all WMU organizations. Then year by year mission volunteers will step out from these YWAs, GAs, and Sunbeam Bands to carry the message of hope to those who seek but cannot find, for they do not know the way.

*Taking stock of fostering.* By what yardstick shall Woman's Missionary Union measure its fostering program? For all these years the majority of societies have been willing to rock along without asking any questions, apparently satisfied with the status quo. Perhaps these questions will help in measuring what is being done:

Are all ages being reached equally well by the organizations? Is there a larger percentage of available Juniors than Intermediates in Girls' Auxiliary? More sixteen- and seventeen-year-olds in YWA than those eighteen to twenty-five? What about Beginners and Primaries?

Are as many boys in proportion to girls from birth through eight being reached in Sunbeam Bands?

Is there an increasing proportion of the prospects being reached each year? If half of the youth (ages fifteen, sixteen, seventeen) were reached last year, has the proportion grown to two thirds now? If one third of the eight-year-olds was enrolled last year, are half of them being reached now?

Are leaders using the mission study books and program materials in the organization meetings in ways that give a balanced attention to all phases of missions? Or are only certain areas and subjects dealt with and the others omitted altogether? Is missions overseas stressed more than missions at home? Stewardship never considered, or, if so, only superficially? All mission areas covered in seasons of prayer?

Are the leaders of the organizations making the most of their opportunities for increasing youth's missionary knowledge and outreach through weekly meetings? Are they meeting only once a month? Twice a month? Or every week? Materials planned and published in *The Window, Tell,* and *Sunbeam Activities* are based on weekly meetings. Is your church making full use of this program for weekly meetings of these weekday missionary organizations?

These questions could serve as the agenda for a full WMU executive committee meeting where all youth directors will be in attendance prior to launching the work for the next promotional year.

Smooth-running machinery is not sufficient for a missionary organization. It is altogether possible for a Woman's Missionary Society to be so absorbed in mechanics that it fails to do its missionary work in regard to youth organizations. If its fostering is going well, one may be quite sure that the society has pushed back its horizons to include the whole world in its interests; that sacrificial giving marks its membership; that intercessory prayer lies at the heart of its spiritual life; that "its own flesh and blood" will be dedicating their lives for full-time missionary service.

5

# Youth and Woman's Missionary Union Ideals

In the center of the purpose of Woman's Missionary Union are five fundamental principles. The Woman's Missionary Society calls them chief aims; YWA and GA refer to them as ideals; Sunbeam Band does not name them formally but every unit of study embraces them. These ideals are the strength of Woman's Missionary Union. They make the organization a *Union.* John C. Calhoun said of this country,

"I never use the word nation in speaking of the United States. I always use the word Union. We are not a nation but a union, a confederacy of sovereign states."

So it is with Woman's Missionary Union. Different in size and strength, and with variety in age, each organization holds at its center the same purpose and the same means for accomplishing this purpose. Through a knowledge of the missionary message of the Bible, a study of missions around the world, the sharing of money, a deepening of the prayer life, and witnessing in the community where one lives, Woman's Missionary Union seeks to promote Christian missions among the children, young girls, and women in every Southern Baptist church.

**Missionary Message of the Bible**

The great theme of the Bible is missionary in character. God's plan for worldwide redemption is the heart of his written Word. Without a knowledge of the Bible's primary message there can be no deeply anchored motive for the modern-day proclamation of the gospel. The lukewarm attitude of members in a Woman's Missionary Society can often be traced to a lack of conviction about sin and its consequences. There would have been no necessity for a universal plan of salvation if sin were not a reality. Man's need determined God's dealing with him and the first missionary promise, Genesis 3:15, was given.

Two thousand years or more went by. Man continued in sin; he was far from God. At this point in history, there was a change in God's method but not in his purpose. He chose Abraham to be the father of an elect people through whom he would bless all mankind. During the period in Egypt and under the leadership of Moses, the Hebrews felt that God was related to them as a people. Throughout the turbulent period of the judges they still had a sense of God's special mission for them. When Israel became a nation, God was at its center. From the beginning to the end of this period of nationhood it is significant that God's revelation of himself was constantly widening.

After the division of the kingdom, followed the period of prophets through whom God revealed his universal character. No more exciting period in history has been recorded than the invasion of Palestine by the Assyrian and Babylonian armies who carried away into captivity these chosen people of God. Idolatry was destroyed. The Jews took the worship of Jehovah into the land of their captors. It was during this period that God's love for all mankind began to be clearly revealed. Suffering Israel was God's servant among the nations and from Israel would come the Suffering Servant, the coming One who would be not only their deliverer but the Saviour of the world.

When the Jews returned to the homeland they were inclined to become introspective and forget that God's redemptive plan included others. Before the closing of the Old Testament canon, God made clear in books like Jonah and Ruth that his love for mankind was worldwide.

With the coming of Jesus, to whom all past events in the Old Testament had pointed, God's purpose was rapidly unfolding. Jesus made it clear that he had come into the world not to condemn the world but to save it. By his supreme sacrifice on Golgotha's hill Jesus paid for the sins of mankind and God's universal love was demonstrated. After the cross came the resurrection, the ascension, and the coming of the Holy Spirit. The young church was ablaze with the good news of the risen Jesus of Nazareth who *is* the gospel. Early believers went everywhere preaching the living word, Jesus Christ.

There were still lessons to be learned about this universal plan for man's salvation. The apostles had to shake off their narrow conception of the kingdom and God's love. It was then that Christianity took a different turn. With the conversion of Saul of Tarsus the good news came to the Gentiles and began its long westward trek. Paul wrote thirteen letters to these mission churches and through them Christendom has come into a knowledge of God's purpose through Jesus Christ and his church that is reassuring, convincing, and profound.

The Bible comes to an end with John's Revelation. God will unify the nations, the King of kings and Lord of lords will come again triumphant over sin as shouts of victory fill the air: "Alleluia! Salvation and glory and power belong to our God; for his judgments are true and just" (Rev. 19:1-2*a* Phillips).

The Bible is essentially a missionary book. It assures man that he is of supreme worth to God. This is a day when a large part of humanity is struggling toward freedom. In spite of man's efforts to stand upright and walk as one made in the image of God, there are worldwide forces which continue to belittle human personality. Life itself is disregarded in the greed of nations. Power-mad men would plunge the world into another war for material gain. Yet God places such value on every Marxist, every African, every Jew, every Asian, every American, every inhabitant of every corner of the globe that he has died that they might have life with freedom to choose and be and grow spiritually toward abundant life.

The Bible tells man where he is going and why. Is man a mere "insignificant incident on the rim of the universe"? Despair is at the end of this road if one cannot find a motive beyond and outside of himself for living. This "beat generation" which feeds on pessimism and a completely secular philosophy of life needs to open the Bible first to the passages which reveal man to himself as he is—insignificant, of little importance, rebellious because of failure to find worthy ends for which to live. Then he makes the further discovery that the Bible exalts man; glorifies the importance of life; gives him the place of pre-eminence in creation. He will discover that man is a spiritual being; that when his body returns to the ground, the spirit returns to God who gave it.

The Bible points to the future. To discover eternity in the midst of time is to find a purpose working toward divine fulfilment. This age is only a part of the ages. Whether this is the last age should matter little in how Christians meet the challenge of today. In the midst of pessimism and the threat of war, with the prospect of total annihilation of the peoples of the earth, one deep look into the purposes of God as they are set forth in the Bible gives assurance of an eternally worthy destiny for mankind. It is this good news that makes the Bible the one indispensable volume on humanity's bookshelf.

### World Awareness

"People who are alive, who find everything interesting, are the people who have developed a high degree of awareness," wrote the editor of the magazine, *House Beautiful*. They have learned not only to look, but to see with perception. The question comes up, are people born with a sense of awareness? Yes, they are. All children have it in abundance. Most adults lose it along the way because they do not use what they have.

There are three stages of awareness, suggested the editor. First, observation. Taking notice. Looking at a thing. Not staring dreamily at something, but real scrutiny of an object: how it is made, what is the design. Take two figures, for example, one made in Mexico, the other on an Indian reservation in the Southwest. Is there any difference? Are they alike? Does the shape of a country on a map stand out in clear detail? Can Malaya be recognized from Vietnam if they are reproduced apart from a map of Asia?

The second stage is insight and understanding. This is seeing with perception. One sees beyond the object to its use and the people who will use it. The

Indian shapes a piece of pottery and decorates it with an original design of wind, rain, and mountains, carves a Kachina doll, or weaves the Kachina mother in the pattern of a basket. It is art, arresting in color and shape, but not art alone, for in the objects is reflected the spirit of worship inherent in the Indian. The oriental bowl with the lotus blossom is not merely a bowl with a lovely flower which may serve a useful purpose, but here is a symbol of Buddhism suggesting perfection and purity claimed as attributes of this ancient Eastern religion. Being able to connect things and see them in interrelationships is progress in awareness.

At this stage of awareness one comes into some understanding of man's conduct. We learn to connect what we read about the past with what is happening in the world today. A knowledge of the way of life of a people includes their religion which is built into the very structure of every society. Some light is shed on the Middle East conflicts by knowing that the two men who have largely dominated that area of the world for many years, Ben-Gurion of Israel and Nasser of Egypt, have moved according to the divergent ethics of Judaism and Islam. A cold isolated fact takes on meaning with insight when there is connection made between an event and what caused the incident. It is at this point one becomes aware of causes and effects.

Someone has said that it is not possible to understand another's religion until one gets a new insight into his own. He sees then the inadequacy of the so-called higher ethnic religions and how deluding is the little core of truth in them. A study of God's redemptive plan for all people as revealed in the Bible, and the knowledge that man has an innate urge for something outside of himself gives insight into other religions. Information alone cannot bring about this understanding.

Participation is the third stage in awareness. When youth has been guided by skilled, dedicated, inspired leadership they see beyond curios, maps, and books to the people. Christian young people have not been educated in missions if they can look at people who know nothing of God's love and still feel no impulse to enter into partnership with God. To see and feel, then to do nothing leaves a void which outlives the situation which produces it. It is not enough to pray, "God, make me aware," but add "God, make me a participant."

Missionary programs, stories, and articles in the WMU magazines, *Tell, Sunbeam Activities, The Window,* and *Royal Service* are roads to travel in world awareness. Through them the youth and their leaders in Woman's Missionary Union are introduced to the people with whom Southern Baptists are working throughout the world. Books for study and reading are more roads for youth to travel in world awareness. Through them they look at the world and if they are led by women who have also looked at the world with insight, it is logical to expect participation on the part of youth.

Through reading mission books young people can have experiences so real that they forget where they are; experiences that take them back into the past as they follow Judson, Carey, Moffat, Morrison, Yates, Mary Slessor; to more recent years in the lives of Rufus Gray, Theron Rankin, and William Wallace; experiences that they could never crowd into a lifetime for the lack of time, money, and maybe capacity.

Without leaving the comfortable nook in the library or the home, young people can be brought, through mission books, into contact with real people all over the world in every condition the imagination of their active minds can conceive. There is death due to superstition; poverty and illness, because of ignorance; bloodshed, for lack of understanding. There is persecution for the devout who will not bow to Caesar; marvelous stories of grace about Christians who witness tirelessly to the truth of the gospel. There are tangled jungles to penetrate with an intrepid missionary; an airplane to fly with a messenger of the Cross. There are roads to travel by cart, rivers to cross in canoes, mountains to climb on foot—in pursuit of men, women, and children who have not heard the good news that Christ died to save them from what they daily experience.

By awakening and deepening the emotions and by giving facts and ideas without which there could be no emotional response, the mission book enormously stimulates youth to want an active part in spreading the gospel.

The leaders of youth should be students of world missions. Today there is no room for the counselor or leader who is too busy with "things" to look at her world. There is no end to the making of books. Thousands of new titles appear in the trade magazines during a year. The question is, what is worth reading? Books that give information on world affairs, that help the adult to understand and appreciate peoples of different cultures and to properly evaluate them, are necessary background reading for a study of books on missions. There are many such books available, but not all of them are equally helpful. The leader's own attitude will determine largely what kind of book in this category of background reading she wants.

This is a good time to point out clearly that "there is no such thing as an interesting book: there can only be interested readers." An incentive to read what has never before had appeal is now rooted in a new purpose: to lead youth to become spiritually aware of their world. Already it has been pointed out that one cannot give what one does not have! This new purpose will make life seem full and reading will become a search, a challenge, and an adventure.

Many of these books are to be found in public and school libraries and are not mission books per se but are books with missionary implications. In the selection of titles leaders may refer to the *WMS Round*

*Table Booklist* and to the reference section in *The World in Books* as well as to the *YWA Book Club List.*

Books for study and reading recommended for Sunbeam Bands, Girls' Auxiliaries, and Young Woman's Auxiliaries are listed in *The World in Books.* YWA members are offered extra reading opportunities through the YWA Book Club. These books selected from the *YWA Book Club List* provide the young women with reading experiences which will give them a comprehensive understanding of missions.

A book is a powerful influence. Lenin at sixteen read and reread Marx's *Manifesto of the Communist Revolution.* Thirty-five years later he was supreme dictator over 150 million Russians and leader of the Communist revolution movement which has plagued free peoples across the world. Voltaire in the early years of young manhood read an atheistic book and it marked his thinking throughout the days of his life. Today there are strong evidences that France has never recovered from that period "when atheists were preachers and mad men were lawgivers." While in prison in South Africa, Gandhi read Tolstoy's *My Religion,* Ruskin's *Unto This Last,* Thoreau's *Essay on Civil Disobedience,* and the *Sermon on the Mount.* These immortal classics gave him light for the rest of his lifework.

The power of the Bible as a missionary force has been demonstrated throughout the centuries. In the interior of India, seventeen years after the Bible had been published in Bengali, missionaries discovered that the people whom they thought had never heard the gospel knew about it. A native said:

"Come and see. The people in the next village have had the good news for a long time. They have given up their idols and they never lie, for they say it is against what their Book teaches."

The missionaries followed the man to another village where they were shown a worn Bible in a wooden box. It was one of Carey's first translations.

The Bible can do for the youth in the organizations of Woman's Missionary Union what it did for the villages in India—change lives and send out youth in glad service. Youth cannot come to intelligent convictions, followed by personal dedication regarding the world mission of Christians, if they are not informed about it. And the basic knowledge is in the Bible.

As Fulton Oursler expresses it, "In this one Book are the two most interesting personalities in the whole world—God and yourself. Read it with your mind awake, your heart open, your soul afire and you will find hope and treasure, and an eternal new world."

### Community Missionary Concern

It is said that Confucius gave his pupils one corner of an idea, expecting them to find the other three. An awareness of world needs is one corner of the basic missionary aims of Woman's Missionary Union. Once leaders and young people have felt the crushing weight of the lostness of mankind, they will find the remaining corners of community concern, stewardship, and prayer.

Telling people by life and word how to be saved from sin is the business of Christians. Across the seas the word is missions; in the homeland it is evangelism; in the individual church the word is soul-winning. All have the same purpose: winning the lost to Christ as Saviour. Upon the members of Woman's Missionary Union rests the obligation to witness in the community as well as in Korea. Youth along with women have the same opportunities for service at home as the missionary has on his field. This mission obligation is an integral part of world missions and is rightly called community missions, thus rounding out the missions cycle.

The primary business of community missions is the salvation of the lost. Manifesting Christian fellowship in the alleviation of suffering among both the unsaved and needy Christians, and the strengthening of Christian standards are also an important part of the mission work in the community where one lives.

Long before the organization of Woman's Missionary Union, Baptist women and young people in mission societies were sewing for the destitute, packing mission barrels, teaching the Bible to Negroes on the plantations, and arranging for "monthly preaching" in needy sections of a given county. Later were added such ministries as holding service in jails and hospitals, doing relief work, visiting in the interest of the church, working among immigrants, and distributing good literature. As the years passed, a vision of what could be done in the community was enlarged. Never has the original intent changed. The primary reason for all humane ministries is that "souls might be clothed with righteousness, prisoners told of release from sin, the sick to be cheered and comforted, strangers to be welcomed and led to better beliefs."

The leadership of youth should face squarely the question of community concern. Actually there can be no adequate education of youth in missions apart from it. Again character insight is essential in order to capitalize on the immediate interests of each age. Adolescents can campaign against obscene literature on the newsstands. In some cities they have appealed to parents to put pressure on operators who violate the law.

They can work in the field of alcohol education. There is a law in each state making a study of facts about alcohol and narcotics mandatory in the public schools of the community. Again youth has taken the initiative, urging parents to take action against taverns and other places of vice. Over three thousand high school students in Winnetka, Illinois expressed concern with the problem of drinking, in a letter sent to each parent:

"We strongly feel that there is no reason for a

high school student to drink. There is no social dignity in it. But some parents must feel that there is, because there are parties at which cocktails are served to students. In other cases, parents knowingly let students bring liquor into parties without taking action."

The letter closed by stating that the students could do little to control the problem so they were turning to parents for help, asking them to stop and think.

The livelihood of many towns depends on migrants working nearby in seasonal crops. Here is a ready place for youth to put into practice their concern for people who need Christ. Frequently there is prejudice against the outsiders. Failure to provide room in schools or a playground for children has resulted in ugly demonstrations in some places. Older youth working with their counselors have assumed responsibility in some communities for directing the attention of church leadership to these problems. Helping newcomers to be accepted and to have a feeling of "belonging" worked a blessing in the lives of the young people. They learned to respect and see value in others who had often been called derisively "trailer trash."

If there are overseas students or professional people in the town or community, the door is open to make the contact that may result in a Christian going back to his country not only equipped with the technical knowledge he came to acquire but with a knowledge of God. "A cup of cold water" offered in Christian fellowship can bridge national and racial chasms.

Along with interest in those of a different culture who are in our colleges and research centers, another area for Christlike concern to be shown is in making friendly contacts across the color line. There is no more urgent challenge facing youth today. Inherent in all Christian teachings is respect for the rights and worth of every individual regardless of his color, creed, or nationality. To study about minorities, people who are different from most of the members in WMU organizations, then refuse to do something about them either physically or spiritually, is to show only surface interest in what Southern Baptists call home missions.

The missionaries employed by our Home Mission Board demonstrate that peoples of different races and nationalities can learn to work and worship together, that national differences can be bridged in the Christian community. It is possible and right for Woman's Missionary Union to teach to youth and lead out in the practice of fair treatment and equal justice to all in the community. These are Christian principles that missionary-minded people ought to practice as well as preach.

By his own power, a Christian finds it difficult to love a person of another race as he loves himself. The reason is rooted in a superiority complex—a sin unworthy of a follower of Him who called the

Samaritan a good neighbor and the Gentile a brother.

Jesus took into his heart the publicans, sinners, and social outcasts of his day, including other races. He sat with them, ate with them, and loved them unto his death. He alone is able to constrain his followers to embrace in love the races and nations of the world. Christ told a lawyer that if he wanted to have eternal life he must love the Lord God with all his heart, with all his soul, with all his strength, with all his mind, and his neighbor as himself. "Learn of me" is Christ's invitation to anyone who is in ignorance of the meaning of "thy neighbor."

There is no way to get older young people to see and understand the real meaning of missions apart from their actually witnessing to the non-Christians around them. They need to proclaim the gospel where they are. Leaders are key people in soul-winning. Older Intermediates and YWAs can share in the church's visitation evangelism and should be included.

The Scripture says it was about noon. Jesus being tired is resting a bit on an old well curb. He is alone. As he looks across the plain he sees a woman coming with her water pitcher on her shoulder. She's thirsty all right; but, like many people today, she doesn't know what she is thirsty for. She and the man who sat quietly on the rim of that old well watching her advance knew that she was terribly dissatisfied with her life. But there was something the woman did not know—only Jesus knew that she did not have to continue living in sin. In the conversation that follows, the woman learns three basic facts about salvation: that God takes the initiative; that it is a free gift; that one receives it on condition that she asks for it. "If thou knewest the gift of God, and who it is that saith to thee, Give me to drink; thou wouldest have asked of him, and he would have given thee living water."

And the result? In the joy of her thrilling discovery she leaves her pitcher and hurries back to the village of Sychar.

"Where are you going?" A likely question someone asks who does not know what has taken place.

"I am going to tell my neighbors about a man who has told me everything I ever did. He must be the Christ!" she quickly replied.

"Who will believe *you*? Everybody in this town knows you've been blown about the streets for many years."

But she did not listen. And then the truth of what happened is revealed in this amazing sentence, "Many . . . believed on him because of the word of the woman" (John 4:39 Montgomery).

The invitation is still open. And will be until he comes again. "Ho, every one that thirsteth, come ye to the waters." "If any man thirst, let him come unto me, and drink."

Woman's Missionary Union wants youth to know the supreme good works in community missions—sharing Christ with one who does not have him.

**Stewardship of Possessions**

What does the girl in Intermediate GA think about when she drops her envelope into the offering plate on Sunday morning? Or does she think about it at all? Is giving "something to the church" a habit that is divorced from purpose or worship? The answers to these questions lie in the teaching about stewardship which the young girl has received in the past.

Stewardship means different things to different people. To some the word goes no deeper than raising the church budget. They have experienced no spiritual imagination in visualizing this budget. To others the word has no meaning at all. To Woman's Missionary Union stewardship means missions. And missions needs money.

Woman's Missionary Union emphasizes as a part of its stewardship teaching and practice, not only the giving of the tithe, but how money is acquired, and the use of the nine tenths. Beginning with the Sunbeam Band the stewardship education plans for youth are based on the first fact of stewardship: God is the owner of *everything*. Woman's Missionary Union further affirms that stewardship is concerned with a person's relationship to all things—no exceptions; that God owns the life of the Christian as well as his possessions. It naturally follows that how the Christian accumulates his property and money, and what he does with his current income are a part of his stewardship. Young people need to learn early in life that to make money requires skill and that God gives the "power to get wealth."

Many Christians are responsible for much of the misery in the world today. They have exploited their brothers to make for themselves riches by which they may gratify selfishness. They have paid inadequate wages to their employees; they have robbed the poor and unskilled laborers to provide luxuries for their bodies and food for their stomachs. They have maintained at little cost to themselves slum property recognized as a menace to health and morals in the community. They have made investments which they knew were "shady." They have gambled on the stock markets. They have participated in give-away rackets, worked for the liquor industries, and have run amusement places which contribute not only to the delinquency of adults but of minors also.

It is a violation of Christian ethics to make money at the expense of society or another human being. People are more important than wealth—even wealth given to the church. The conscience of Christians needs to be pricked at this point. There are men of means, some of them Baptists, who openly state that it is nobody's business how they make their money; that they tithe and this practice should satisfy everybody—including critics and conscience.

Young people in WMU organizations are now receiving instruction in basic principles of earning money which are in harmony with the will of God.

It is high time, for, of the present 18 million teen-agers in the United States, 9½ million have some income of their own. The spending power of these teen-agers between thirteen and nineteen years old amounts to $9 billion a year! By 1965 there will be 24 million teen-agers who will be spending $14 billion! The teen-age consumer is a force to be reckoned with.

In stewardship, motive is much more important than amount, for if the motive is right the amount usually takes care of itself. Moving stories of little children starving and pictures of bodies ravished by disease are not sufficient motives for Christian giving. Any decent person will make his gift in the name of philanthropy when appealed to for humanity's sake. Gratitude to God for what he has done in reaching down to man and lifting him out of his sin is the Christian's best reason for giving. To share Christ the Saviour with the rest of the world is the natural expression of his gratitude. This is missions. It is this purpose that Woman's Missionary Union seeks to implant in the minds and hearts of the youth in the WMU organizations.

How much to give, logically follows the motive for giving. How much *shall* it be? Woman's Missionary Union has always taught that the tithe is the minimum. The Bible teaches tithing. It was practiced long before the Ten Commandments were given on Sinai. Christ, our high priest after the order of Melchizedek, still receives the tithe. Nowhere in the New Testament is the tithe set aside or discredited. Tithing is not taught youth in order that they may expect financial returns or to solace a guilty conscience. They are taught tithing because it is right. All youth in the WMU organizations are encouraged to give the tithe through their churches.

Knowing that Bible stewardship includes tithes and offerings, Woman's Missionary Union has always promoted "over and above" gifts. The Lottie Moon Christmas Offering for Foreign Missions and the Annie Armstrong Offering for Home Missions, as well as state mission offerings, are recognized throughout the denomination as second only to the Cooperative Program dollars in amount and usefulness to the cause of missions.

Through stewardship education plans, programs in the magazines, and suggested books to study, youth in Sunbeam Band, Girls' Auxiliary, and Young Woman's Auxiliary are made aware of what their money will do and where it goes. They learn why they should contribute their money to the total financial program. They learn that through the Cooperative Program they can witness in distant places, that they are having a part in all the work that Southern Baptists are doing for Christ and the world; that this is a personal way in which they can share in the Great Commission.

A significant part of stewardship education plans for youth includes a second look at the nine tenths. To be sure, offerings are a portion of the nine tenths, but caring Christians will look at not only the amount they give but how much they have left and what they are doing with it. A high standard of living does not necessarily mean owning every new gadget that comes along. Since World War II Americans have spent $15 billion on TV sets, and in a recent year $10 billion on automobiles, $10 billion on liquor, $5 billion on tobacco, $1½ billion on jewelry, $1½ billion on candy, $1 billion for toilet goods, soap not included, $500 million on dogs, $200 million on fishing tackle for sport. "Everybody has them" is the cry. This is no real reason. Most of these "things" are prestige items and are wanted not because they are needed but because they give "place" to those who do not have them.

The story goes that at a banquet for Mark Antony, Cleopatra stunned her guests by showing them an enormous pearl of absolute perfection. One by one the guests held it with awe for it was valued in today's currency at three-fourths of a million dollars. When it was handed back to her she dropped it into a glass of vinegar, waited while it dissolved and then drank it with a gesture of arrogance. Christians who are gasping as they read of such frivolous vulgarity and complete disregard for values should look again at the expenditures of Americans in these recent years. Youth along with their elders should learn to discipline their desires and buy wisely with their nine tenths.

No one but God can tell a person what he should

do with his money. But no one is left in the uncertainty of silence, for God has told his children in his Word specifically about tithes and offerings and in general about the broad principles that govern the getting and using of wealth. His spoken word is as near as the Bible.

A stewardship truth of profound significance that should be explained to all young people is that money is *not* filthy lucre but stored up personality, sacred and powerful. This is the reason the youth in WMU organizations should be led to earn their money. They can quickly understand that the dollar in their hand represents the physical, mental, and emotional energy that went into the earning of that dollar. It is the real "I." Through money the youth is released and can be multiplied a thousand times as his coined personality touches the four corners of the earth.

Giving is at the heart of Christianity. "For God so loved the world, that he gave his only begotten Son, that whosoever believeth in him should not perish, but have everlasting life" (John 3:16). Giving is tied in with the definition of missionary education—a Christlike concern.

God's point of view can be approximated only when through some personal experience Christlike interest in somebody else is shown. The little child helping a birdling back into its nest or protecting it from harm is manifesting an attitude that is akin to divine love. It is at this point that leaders of

Sunbeam Bands are cultivating the parental heart that is in every human being and is basic to a later understanding of God as our Father, who loved so much that he gave his son that the helpless and lost ones may find him.

It is a far cry from this concept of giving to the patent announcement made by a leader to her organization, "Don't forget to bring your offering tomorrow." But the gap need not be so great. Giving is not only for the purpose of supporting missionaries and institutions; it is a means of expressing the purpose of God and of sharing with him in the extension of the kingdom.

**Prayer**

And now the remaining corner of the great idea known as the chief aims of Woman's Missionary Union—prayer, the mightiest missionary force in the world.

Nineteen hundred years of missionary experience have proved that prayer and missions are inseparably linked. The book of Acts reminds twentieth-century Christians of the place given to united prayer in the expansion of the kingdom. That first New Testament church did not begin with articles of incorporation or a committee to draw up goals, but in a prayer meeting. These early Christians knew how to pray. They were willing to wait *with one accord* in prayer for God to speak to them. And he did.

In that day the strength of concerted prayer had

to be rooted in the power of secret personal intercession. It is still true today. With this concept of prayer in mind Woman's Missionary Union lays emphasis on individual and united prayer for all of its members.

Baptist women have chattered too long through every religious experience. The moment the voice stops they become self-conscious. The mind wanders. This is distressing. F. W. Faber's words are worth pondering: "In spirituality talking is always a loss of power. It is like steam. It is mighty when it is imprisoned, a mere vapour when it is set free."

Spiritual realities do not shout to be heard and it is still true that Jesus comes "the door being shut." There are moments when the soul knows communion with God and, alone with him, experiences peace and power. To keep on listening in the depth of spiritual sound may give the person deeper insight into human nature than a year's contact with people. This is why the great solitaries know so much about life. They know man because they know God and have heard his voice. Self-deception is the most formidable enemy of the spiritual life and the last to be conquered. There is no better cure for it than silence with God.

But prayer is something else, too. It is a long, hard road from self to God; from loving self to loving God. Many new methods of prayer which profess to deliver the Christian from self are but subtle variations of the self-centered prayer. Some of the prayer cults urge concentration on God in order to obtain spiritual power. Actually the motive is to gain relief from trouble. God is not the end, only the means. This does not mean that petition is to be excluded from prayer, but it does mean that there is a higher motive than seeking help in personal problems. The motive will be to get nearer to God, to know him better, to enter more fully into his thoughts and purposes.

Much of the difficulty in prayer would disappear if the Christian realized the simple truth that "prayer is dying to self and becoming alive unto God." Self dies slowly. When God begins to tear out self-love from the heart, then and then only is the Christian aware of the depth of it. Self-confidence is gone; thoughts and words take their leave; the heart is cold. God has withdrawn his hand and the feeling of desolation is complete. The temptation to give up the journey is never greater. But this is the darkness before the dawn. In withdrawing his presence the full realization comes that without him the Christian can do nothing. To walk through the slough of spiritual despondency and be willing to turn the empty heart to God in a childlike "movement of love" is to make a great discovery—God *is*. No words are necessary. The roots of self-love have been cut but it takes eternal vigilance to keep them from sprouting again!

It is this power in the individual life of the woman that is meant when Woman's Missionary Union talks about "missionary praying." It is to labor the point to go beyond this statement: Everything that takes place in a Sunbeam Band, Girls' Auxiliary, and Young Woman's Auxiliary is colored by the leadership's conception of the purpose of prayer. No matter what the words sound like, no matter how perfect the discipline, no matter how effective the program, no matter how heavy the cross she may be bearing to assume the responsibility, self-glorification may taint everything she does.

This conception of the leader will be reflected by the spirit in which the calendar of prayer is observed. In many meetings "observed" is the correct word. It is not the method or manner that should be under scrutiny—we have novel enough ways—but the spirit in which prayer is made. The counselor or leader reflects in that short period whether her life is self-centered or alive unto God. Sobering to the point of being frightening is this plea of a missionary couple: "We can no more live in Africa without your prayers than we can survive without food!"

What is true relative to praying for the missionaries on their birthdays is true about the weeks of prayer. They, too, can become routine, a habit, a mere observance. A new departure can be taken in prayer preparation by the leadership which will be made evident in results both as to gifts and to lives offered in service. Go back and look at Paul before he went out on his first missionary journey. "And it came to pass . . . even while I prayed in the temple I was in a trance . . . and he said unto me, depart, for I will send thee far hence unto the Gentiles." None of the leaders in the early days of Christianity dared venture into his work without the preparation of prayer. Since that day every manifestation of a new devotion to missions has been rooted in a revival of prayer. Numbers have not been important—only people who were willing to take time to pray.

The success of the first Christmas offering for foreign missions sprang from the completely dedicated Christ-centered life of Lottie Moon. Not a perfect woman, but one who had self torn out of her life through the long, lonely pilgrimage of denial until she and God walked together. "I would I had a thousand lives that I might give them to the women of China," she cried in deep anguish of soul. This is the spirit that marked the beginning of both weeks of prayer.

Annie Armstrong practiced self-denial long before the home mission offering took that name. For eighteen years without salary she crossed and recrossed the continent making Christ known to men, women and children, irrespective of race, color, or station in life. In her little office in Baltimore she led in writing by hand to those fifteen hundred societies, asking them to make an offering for foreign missions.

The worldwide conception of missions is reflected in both women. Lottie Moon urged not only a week of prayer and offering for foreign missions, but at the same time she suggested that the work of the Home Mission Board be included. Annie Armstrong led the young organization to undertake the first Christmas offering for China. So it was that through the prayer and devotion of these two women with the world in their hearts, spiritual power has gone out to the ends of the earth.

The mission offerings have grown to such proportions that there is grave danger in relying on numbers rather than on prayer to keep the amount still growing. Not recently has there been a great outpouring of the Holy Spirit such as was manifested in previous decades on foreign fields. Nor are there mission volunteers at home in large enough numbers to reach the unsaved hordes that are rapidly increasing, as has already been pointed out. The spiritual tides are running low. The Foreign Mission Board still pleads for recruits. In 1946 the late Dr. M. T. Rankin set a goal of 1,750 foreign service missionaries. Dr. Baker James Cauthen said in 1954 that at the rate Southern Baptists were going it would take twenty-five years longer. Yet in the period from 1954 to 1979 statisticians say there will be added 300 million more people to the world's population.

"The evangelization of the world in this generation depends first of all upon a revival of prayer. Deeper than the need of men; deeper, far, than the need for money; deep down at the bottom of our spiritless life is the need for the forgotten secret of prevailing, worldwide prayer."[1]

At the time of the weeks of prayer, leaders of youth have their greatest opportunities to help these young people find direction for their lives. Again each leader is confronted with the conception she holds of prayer. To let go of self and live for God is not easy. The whole question of vocation is connected with this aspect of prayer. The leader herself may be involved at this point. Many a Christian finds prayer a weariness if not torture because she lacks the courage to face the question as to whether her daily work is in line with the divine plan for her life. Any vocation that runs counter to God's will can prove a hindrance to the spiritual life. Self-will or sheer spineless drifting is every whit and grain as wrong in the kitchen as in the executive suite.

Christians both young and old often find themselves in uncongenial employment simply because they chose it in self-will at a time when it appeared congenial and thought it would always seem so. Perhaps the majority of those who plead uncongenial work, as an excuse for their lack of spiritual joy, could change employment tomorrow if they were willing to pay the price. They are afraid to trust God. Still less can one live for God while engaged in dishonest or questionable occupations. It all goes back to the question: Is God being used as a means of self-realization or is the Christian offering himself as a means of glorifying God?

The leaders of youth have only a short time to guide and stimulate these children and young people. A few years in the future they will see the results of their efforts, either successes or failures. So much depends on the little things that take place in a meeting. Maybe it is a word of praise for a little child who is struggling with block building. Because of the warmth of the leader the child comes to love Sunbeam Band and later recalls the impression made and where it has led in her life. Perhaps it is a suggestion of a new approach to a difficult work that spurs on the young girl to try again in Forward Steps. Or the senior in high school comes to her counselor for help in math or a problem in dating. The encouragement and advice she receives may make all the difference in future decisions. So great are these little everyday affairs that only a leader who has given heart and mind to God through prayer will see in them opportunitics affecting the future of those she leads. One does not have to say a word about faith or doing God's will in many of these personal contacts. It will be evident to the youth in hundreds of ways whether or not the leader walks with God.

### Together with God

Two billion people still unreached and the number increasing rapidly; peace-loving nations attacked or annexed by ruthless aggressors; persecutions, famines, earthquakes, and floods make the Christian ask Gideon's question, "If the Lord be with us, wherefore is all this come upon us?" Look into the mirror of the question and there will be reflected selfish, worldly, unfaithful Christians who have hampered the divine Worker.

It is time to be personal. What does Christianity mean if it doesn't mean that you and I are forgiven for a purpose? It takes power to achieve the purpose. And this power was promised us—the last of the promises that fell from His lips was that we should receive the Holy Spirit, "Lo, I am with you alway, even unto the end of the world." " 'I am' covers all the varieties of *was, is, will be*"; all days regardless of kind—summer, winter, storm, or sunshine, days of youth, and days of old age.

The Holy Spirit follows no prescribed line that man draws. His power falls on a monk in a convent and he brings about the Reformation. His power falls on a tinker in Bedford jail and he writes *Pilgrim's Progress.* His power falls on a cobbler in Kettering and he founds the modern missionary movement. His power falls on a Congregational missionary on his way to the Orient and he comes back to America a Baptist to lead the people into a deeper conception of missions.

His power falls on a Fannie E. S. Heck and she writes into the very life of Woman's Missionary Union plans embracing youth so far reaching "that the years have not yet overtaken them." The Holy Spirit is power—like the wind. The same breath of God which stirs the curtains at an open window with the softest breeze, drives the mighty sea against towering rocks. So it is with the Holy Spirit. He is power—like fire. The fire of God thaws your coldness, makes you glow with enthusiasm, burns up your shallow, flimsy ideas about sin and man's lostness, makes your creed a living power. "If the Spirit dwells in us he will make us fiery like himself."

Yes, it takes power to educate youth in missions
It takes power to lift their hearts to the Lord
And this power comes from being filled with
God's Spirit.
Youth will join maturity and together they shall
Show the Saviour to the nations
And the darkness shall turn to dawning
And dawning to noonday bright
When all of the world's great peoples
Come to the truth of God.

# Notes

## Chapter 1

[1]Carl T. Rowan, *The Pitiful and the Proud* (New York: Random House, Inc., 1956), pp. 55-56. Used by permission.

[2]George F. Kennan, "Foreign Policy and Christian Conscience," *The Atlantic Monthly*, May 1959.

## Chapter 2

[1]James L. Hymes, Jr., *A Child Development Point of View* (New York: Prentice-Hall, Inc., 1955). Used by permission.

[2]*Ibid.*, pp. 81-82.

[3]*Ibid.*, p. 83.

[4]Herbert Carleton Mayer, *Young People in Your Church* (Westwood: Fleming H. Revell, 1953). Used by permission.

[5]Dorothy W. Baruch, *How to Live with Your Teen-Ager* (New York: McGraw-Hill Book Co., 1953). Used by permission.

[6]Peter Fingsten, "Beat and Buddhist," *The Christian Century*, February 25, 1959. Used by permission.

[7]*Ibid.*

## Chapter 3

[1]Nevin C. Harner, *Youth Work in the Church* (Nashville: Abingdon Press, 1942).

## Chapter 4

[1]Richard Rodgers and Oscar Hammerstein, *South Pacific* (New York: Williamson Music, Inc., 1949). Used by permission.

[2]Nina Millen (Editor), *The World from Our Home* (New York: Friendship Press, Inc., 1956). Used by permission.

[3]Ethlene Boone Cox, *Following in His Train* (Nashville: Broadman Press, 1938), p. 157. Used by permission.

[4]Jessie Eleanor Moore, *Missionary Education of Beginners* (Missionary Education Movement of the United States and Canada, 1927). (Out of print)

## Chapter 5

[1]Robert Speer, *Prayer and Missions* (Birmingham: Woman's Missionary Union).

# Bibliography


Adeney, Dand H. *The Unchanging Commission.* Chicago: Inter-Varsity, 1955.

Boer, Harry R. *The World Missionary Situation Today.* Grand Rapids: Eerdmans, 1958.

Friedenberg, Edgar Z. *The Vanishing Adolescent.* Boston: Beacon, 1959.

Harner, Nevin C. and Baker, David D. *Missionary Education in Your Church.* New York: Friendship, 1958.

Kerouac, Jack. "The Roaming Beatniks," *Holiday* (Philadelphia), (October, 1959).

Moraes, Frank. *Yonder One World.* New York: Macmillan, 1958.

Notestein, Frank. "Poverty and Population," *Atlantic Monthly* (New York), (November, 1959).

Stevens, Dorothy. *Missionary Education in a Baptist Church.* Philadelphia: Judson, 1953.

Wyckoff, D. Campbell. *In One Spirit.* New York: Friendship, 1957.

# Questions

## Chapter 1

1. What principle factors have contributed to shrinking the world today?
2. Which characteristic of the world do you consider the most significant to missions?
3. What is your understanding of the term colonialism?
4. What has brought about the change in the modern-day idea of missions?
5. Explain "population explosion."

## Chapter 2

1. State three laws of growth for the child, birth through eight.
2. When does a child's spiritual growth begin?
3. Name five characteristics of the Junior.
4. What are the chief differences between middle and older adolescence?
5. Give your opinion of the modern-day adolescent in the light of "break loose is normal."

## Chapter 3

1. Do you agree with the reasons given for too few leaders of youth? Defend your position.

2. Do you believe that it makes any serious difference what a leader of youth knows about missions? Give reasons to support your opinion.
3. What is meant by "a leader must communicate"?
4. What is the most important characteristic for a leader of youth to possess? Why?
5. How do *you* measure up as a leader of young people in the light of the discussion in this chapter?

Chapter 4

1. Give illustrations of how the home can undergird the missionary education of youth.
2. What is the missionary program of WMU for children, birth through eight, in Baptist churches?
3. Suggest ways in which the work of Young Woman's Auxiliary can be strengthened in your church.
4. In your opinion what are some of the strong points in the program of work for Girls' Auxiliary?
5. Discuss fostering.

Chapter 5

1. What is the missionary message of the Bible?
2. What does "awareness" mean? How is this quality of mind and spirit related to missions?
3. Can a person be "missionary" who fails or refuses to witness to the unsaved in the community? How do you witness for Christ in your community?
4. State the position of Woman's Missionary Union in regard to the stewardship of possessions?
5. What is your conception of prayer?
6. Write a paragraph on "Why I believe in educating the young people in my church in missions."

Edna Mae Humes
Sharon Lynn Agee (April 6, 1963
Mary James April 1963
Alice Agee Aug-26-1963